W9-BLL-728

MOUNTAIN WOLF WOMAN

SISTER OF CRASHING THUNDER

The Autobiography of a Winnebago Indian

MOUNTAIN WOLF WOMAN

SISTER OF CRASHING THUNDER

The Autobiography of a Winnebago Indian

Edited by Nancy Oestreich Lurie
Foreword by Ruth Underhill

ANN ARBOR PAPERBACKS
THE UNIVERSITY OF MICHIGAN PRESS

FOURTH PRINTING 1974

FIRST EDITION AS AN ANN ARBOR PAPERBACK 1966

COPYRIGHT © BY THE UNIVERSITY OF MICHIGAN 1961

ALL RIGHTS RESERVED

ISBN 0-472-09109-3 (CLOTHBOUND)

ISBN 0-472-06109-7 (PAPERBOUND)

PUBLISHED IN THE UNITED STATES OF AMERICA BY

THE UNIVERSITY OF MICHIGAN PRESS AND SIMULTANEOUSLY

IN DON MILLS, CANADA, BY LONGMAN CANADA LIMITED

MANUFACTURED IN THE UNITED STATES OF AMERICA

To the Memory of

Carl Ralph Oestreich

and

James Sydney Slotkin

 **FOREWORD**

BY RUTH UNDERHILL

In early monographs that aimed to map and relate the patterns of American Indian life, women often appeared merely as links in the kinship system. The ceremonial spotlight caught them briefly at their high points of puberty, childbirth and widowhood and the economic spotlight when their marriages were arranged and paid for. Otherwise they formed, in most cases, an undifferentiated mass of workers, excluded from council and, often, from ceremonies.

True, women could be shamans in California and, in lesser degree, in some other areas. True, the women of Plains and Pueblos had some ceremonies of their own. Still, even in matrilineal and matrilocal societies, the main figures in war, government and ceremony were men. So were the ethnologists who studied them. Even our major women writers, toward the century's beginning, had their chief rapport with male ceremonialists. *Vide* Matilda Stevenson with the Zuni, Alice Fletcher with Pawnee and Omaha, and Frances Densmore with her many studies of Indian music.

As our knowledge of Indian lifeways increased, there was need for more light and shade in the general picture. Verbatim accounts by informants became more usual and many of these were by women. Parsons, Opler and Spier, for instance, found the housewife's memory of day-to-day events often more complete than her husband's. A growing interest in economic life brought more descriptions of female craft workers.

The talkative, characterful women who thus appeared were not the colorless drudges some writers had assumed. Nor were they romantic figures like the legendary "princesses" who made so many cliffs famous by leaping over them when crossed in love. In most cases, the Indian woman's life appeared very like that of our pioneer great-grandmothers. Her work, like theirs, was done apart from the men. At gatherings, men and women formed separate groups, as they still do at country socials. In fact, a woman's work and play were mostly with children and with other women. This is the case in most primitive societies, while our own more sophisticated and romantic form of behavior is a comparatively recent development.

Even yet, we are inclined to judge the Indian woman's life by these modern standards. If we are to see her as living a full life in her own sphere, studies in depth are needed and will be for some time. Michelson (1933) gave the curt account which was all an Arapaho woman felt inclined to tell. Gladys Reichard, in Dezba, painted a sympathetic picture of a Navaho matriarch, from a white woman's point of view. In the same year, I collected the disjointed statements of an ancient Papago woman, too old to organize and tell a connected story. In 1959, Carmen Lee Smithson published a detailed account of life among Havasupai women, though not in their own words. Nancy Lurie's tape recording of the year-by-year experiences of a Winnebago woman thus far stands almost alone as source material for a woodland Indian woman's activities and attitudes.

Mountain Wolf Woman, her heroine, was the sister of Crashing Thunder whose story was published by Radin thirty-five years ago. Both shared the same period of Winnebago acculturation but the difference between them is immense.

Crashing Thunder is not strictly an autobiography, although every word in it came out of the Indian's mouth. Rather, it is a drama, centering around a religious experience. From the jumble of reminiscences which anyone pours out when talking about himself, one feels that the ethnologist has selected first, those bearing on religious education and myths, then the fall to drunkenness and murder, and finally, the salvation through peyote. This cult, which had only recently worked its way up from the south, featured visions which could lead to achievement. However, the visions were not produced by ordeals in the old manner, but by eating a cactus with hallucinatory properties. His vision achieved, Crashing Thunder's drama closes, though he has lived some forty years since then. Here Radin was artist rather than ethnologist—and why not? He had already described Winnebago customs in another volume.

Mountain Wolf Woman's life is handled very differently. No particular pattern appears other than the slow change from the life of an illiterate Indian food gatherer to that of a responsible church member who lives in a modern house, travels in Pullman trains, and believes in the Christian Heaven. The story was recorded on tape, exactly as it flowed from the informant's lips. Mountain Wolf Woman does not describe scenes nor explain relationships and customs. She expects these to be understood as they would be by an Indian audience. Dr. Lurie did understand. She has supplied copious notes, without which the reader would be lost. Occasionally, some episode was transferred to a different place in the story, at the speaker's own request. Otherwise there is no editing or intrusion of psychological analysis. However, the factual notes make Mountain Wolf Woman's background so clear that we can infer her reactions and attitudes almost as if she were present before us.

Dr. Lurie is to be thanked for this opportunity of day-by-day acquaintance with a woodland Indian woman.

✌ PREFACE

Autobiographies are published for a variety of reasons. Authors often disclaim any personal importance but justify making their memoirs public because of close association with the great people and stirring events of their time. Individuals whose roles are of obvious historical significance frequently explain that a sense of social responsibility requires that they make known the underlying influences and motivations of their actions. Mountain Wolf Woman has told her story for a reason that is at once simpler and more complex than those usually adduced. Her niece asked for the story. Among the Winnebago Indians, a strong sense of obligation to relatives prevails, as well as the reciprocal sense of right to call upon them as the need or desire for favors may arise. The fact that the kinship in this case is one of adoption and not of blood makes it no less binding from a Winnebago point of view.

Our relationship stems from my adoption by Mountain Wolf Woman's parallel cousin, Mitchell Redcloud, Sr. According to Winnebago reckoning, they are classified as brother and sister because their fathers were brothers. Thus, Mountain Wolf Woman is my aunt. I had met Redcloud during the summer of 1944 in the course of my first field work among the Winnebago. When I began my senior year at the University of Wisconsin the following fall, I learned that Redcloud was a cancer patient at the Wisconsin General Hospital on the university campus. I visited him frequently and my questions about Winnebago culture helped relieve the tedium of existence in a hospital ward. In time he came to believe that our association had been preordained. Despite frequent and intense periods of pain, Redcloud forced himself to instruct me as fully as possible about his people, even writing long accounts of Winnebago customs to present to me when I appeared during hospital visiting hours. He was eventually scheduled for surgery, and fearing that he might not survive the operation, presented me with a cherished and valuable legacy—adoption as his daughter. I thus acquired a Winnebago name, a clan affiliation, and a host of relatives upon whom I could rely in continuing the task Redcloud and I had begun. Redcloud's condition precluded the traditional announcement of such an adoption at a public feast, but he did write of it to Mountain Wolf Woman and evidently told other Winnebago during the year he lived following the operation.

Thus, when I met Mountain Wolf Woman in the summer of 1945 while working at the Winnebago community of Black River Falls, Wisconsin, she greeted me as her niece. My aunt soon proved to be not only a valuable informant, but a good friend as well. Her personality and her own experiences as an individual became as interesting to me as the ethnographic data about the Winnebago which she could provide. I felt that her autobiography would be of great interest both as a literary document and as a source of insights for anthropological purposes. I was inspired, naturally, by the fact that the first full-length autobiography of an American Indian edited and published by an anthropologist, Paul Radin, had been that of a Winnebago, Crashing Thunder. The example set by Radin in 1920 has been followed by the publication of a number of autobiographies of American Indians and other native peoples. However, few such life histories have been collected from women. Therefore, Mountain Wolf Woman's story takes on particular significance in scholarly terms, since it is the account of a woman from the same tribe as Crashing Thunder. However, I knew Mountain Wolf Woman almost a year before I learned that she is the sister of Crashing Thunder. Thus, a unique opportunity was presented to obtain an autobiography which would be valuable not only for its own sake but also for its comparative importance in regard to Radin's work.

Mountain Wolf Woman readily agreed to my request for her story, but a great deal of time elapsed before we could actually begin work on the project. In the first place, I realized that a request of such magnitude would require a commensurate gift as a matter of reciprocal kin obligations. I was obliged for many years to use any field funds I received for more general research on the Winnebago. Then there were technical problems. Mountain Wolf Woman's household was crowded with small grandchildren she was rearing and she did not have the leisure or quiet to write her story in the Winnebago syllabary script, let alone in English which she would find even more difficult. Furthermore, I was fully occupied for several years with teaching and other research.

It was not until 1957 that I could begin to give serious thought to the long-delayed work with Mountain Wolf Woman. By that time she was able to put her household in the temporary charge of an adult grandaughter in order to stay with me. Thanks to the Rackham Fund for Faculty Research of The University of Michigan and to the Bollingen Foundation, grants-in-aid were provided to finance the project.

I notified Mountain Wolf Woman that work could begin and she traveled from her home at Black River Falls to Milwaukee where I met her and accompanied her on the rest of her journey to Ann Arbor, Michigan. This incident is duly noted in her autobiography as it was her first airplane flight. We worked together at my home for almost five weeks during January and February of 1958.

We began our task by discussing the best manner of procedure. She soon became accustomed to using a tape recorder and decided she preferred it to writing her story in the Winnebago syllabary script that her brother had employed. She also chose to speak Winnebago rather than English as it allowed for easier recall and discussion of events. However, to aid me in the task of translation, she repeated the entire story on tape in English using the Winnebago recordings as a guide. Since the account was told directly to me, it was natural for Mountain Wolf Woman to gloss over details of Winnebago culture and history. I have therefore made notes for each chapter providing more extensive data on matters which may be of further interest to the reader. The first day's work proved highly disconcerting to me. Mountain Wolf Woman told her entire story on less than half a reel of tape. Although I endeavored to hide my feelings, my disappointment must have been evident since she observed that the story could be made much longer on the basis of the many notes I had made in conversations with her during earlier periods of field work. I said that I would really like to hear all the stories again to be sure that I had understood them correctly. A knowing smile crossed her face and she said, "This is just a start to show where we will go, like beginning of a book."

She began her story again, eliminating what she recognized as meaningless details, expanding and adding events more pertinent to her own experiences. She recounted episodes already familiar to me and many new ones.

The completed autobiography thus consists of the second

or long account of Mountain Wolf Woman's life, supplemented where necessary from the shorter account or from other data such as the English version of the narrative or comments made in the course of our work but not transcribed on the tapes. Where such additions have been made in the text, they are preceded by a dash (—) and if they occur within a sentence or exceed a single sentence are followed by (—). The first or brief account appears as Appendix A at the end of the book and the reader may thus note which additions in the main text were taken from the first account.

The transcription of Mountain Wolf Woman's story was doubtless one of the most pleasant ways imaginable of doing "field work." Mountain Wolf Woman is a delightful companion, witty, empathic, intelligent and forthright. During the course of our work she thought of herself as a visiting relative. When my teaching schedule interrupted our work, she found ways to occupy her time, and even between daily recording sessions she was never idle. Indeed, she is incapable of idleness and equates personal contentment with useful activity. She sewed clothing for herself, and even split wood for the fireplace when she felt in need of exercise. Because my birthday occurred during the course of her visit she decided to make me a gift in the form of elaborate floral beading of the buckskin dress I wear for lectures of a popular nature, explaining, "The girls wearing fancier dresses to powwows nowdays."

She looked upon our main task as fun rather than work, although she expressed surprise that "just talking" could be so physically tiring, and confided that she never appreciated that I must really work quite hard as a teacher. However, beds had to be made, dishes washed, and the house put in order each morning before I dared suggest we sit down beside the tape recorder.

Mountain Wolf Woman was pleased to have my study as a room all to herself where she slept and could retire to read, sew or write letters to her children. She also appreciated the fact that our house has running water, but most of our electrical appliances struck her as more trouble than they are worth. She particularly distrusted the electric stove, since she is accustomed to cooking at a wood-burning range or over an open fire out-of-doors. Thus, on days when both my husband and I were away teaching, she chose to prepare her meals at the living room fireplace, even baking bread in the embers as a surprise for us when we returned in the late afternoon. In fact, Mountain Wolf Woman gradually transformed our home into a Winnebago household with activity centered about the fireplace in the living room. The recording equipment was shortly moved from the acoustical isolation of my study to the living room. Consequently, the tapes contain peripheral sounds of doorbell, telephone, cat meows, and my husband's footfalls. However, the greater ease Mountain Wolf Woman felt in working amidst the bustle of daily living more than compensated for these technical imperfections in the recordings.

When telling her story, Mountain Wolf Woman would settle herself comfortably in a large chair, fold her hands in her lap, close her eyes and begin to relive events as she recalled them. Sad incidents often caused tears to well up, and funny stories evoked chuckles.

Mountain Wolf Woman likes to refer to herself as an "old Winnebago lady." This is an accurate self-assessment because among the Winnebago age carries connotations of wisdom and dignity. It also carries the privilege of speaking frankly on the basis of knowledge and understanding derived from observing the world for a long time.

Considered very pretty in her youth, Mountain Woman's face still reflects this basic beauty and the deeper beauty of serene old age. Her dark, expressive face is attractively contrasted with her perfectly white hair, which is always combed straight back into a neat bun. Although she often dresses "like a white lady," she usually wears a style of clothing typical of Winnebago women of her age. This consists of a full cotton skirt topped by a loose, collarless blouse reaching just to the waist. She likes to wear large fringed shawls for special occasions but considers coats and sweaters far more practical for working out-of-doors. Her short stature and style of dress suggest a stolid obesity, but this effect is dispelled by the quick grace of her movements.

Like many Winnebago women, she never wears a hat, but binds a silk kerchief tightly about her hair, bringing the ends together in a neat knot above her forehead. Her ears are pierced and though she now wears earrings only in the lobes, the helices of her ears show small punctate marks. Traditionally, Winnebago women wore five or six pairs of long earrings dependent from the edges of their ears.

Throughout Mountain Wolf Woman's stay I regretted that it was not possible to have a microphone constantly recording her conversation. Our mealtimes and periods of domestic activity were enlivened by her spontaneous observations and comments. Frequent good-natured teasing increased the effect of living in a Winnebago household. Aunts stand in a joking relationship to their nieces' husbands and I had warned my husband that our guest might tease him. She did, accusing him of laziness in providing for her wants in the way of food and firewood. She had never met my husband before her visit to our home and in a moment of serious conversation with me she expressed her approval of him in traditional Winnebago terms, "Kind, a good worker, and not jealous-hearted." However, in talking to him she frequently engaged in the outrageous coquetry appropriate to their relationship. The English term "Honey," as a form of affectionate address amuses Mountain Wolf Woman and so she usually called my husband, "My Honey, Add" (Ed). One night as we watched a television commercial concerning a preparation for coloring hair, she turned seriously toward my husband and mimicking the simpering voice of the young woman on the screen, she asked, "Honey, what color would you like me to dye my hair?"

Television is still a rather novel experience for Mountain Wolf Woman, but she had purchased a set for her own home shortly before coming to visit us. She reasoned shrewdly that since she would not be home to supervise her young grand-daughters, the television set would be an inducement for them to stay home at night. An interesting result of television viewing at Ann Arbor was revealed in a letter from Mountain Wolf Woman upon her return to Black River Falls.

She evidently recalled a program in which small scale models were used to illustrate how the Russians might land an unmanned rocket on the moon. By remote control the rocket disgorged a jeep-like vehicle which rolled about taking pictures and transmitting them back to earth. The presentation was designed to be frightening and I had been properly disturbed by the impersonal awesomeness of such technological speculations. However, Mountain Wolf Woman has lived far longer than I have and has seen the transition from horse to airplane without feeling a sense of threat to her individuality. Her letter, while indicative of her brief schooling, illustrates her remarkable ability to organize new information into meaningful patterns, reducing the extraordinary to comprehensible and even comfortingly amusing terms.

"My dear neice.

"I'm writing to thank you that money you sent me [payment for moccasins and other items I had ordered]. and I'm going to tell you a story. You alway like old story. about the moon. long time ago when the world new old time of different tribe were against each other. that time [a Winnebago] went away from his people when he came back to his home war came and kill whole town and this man he trace them he follow them to and he got to where they come from. he there toward morning. that time indian chief alway live right in middle of the town. he new [knew] where the chief son and his wife. so the peoples were slept real deep. he went in cut chief son head of [off] and his wife too. and he took both heads and went up to the moon. when the moon full moon you could see him he's carry two human head in his hand. his name is Sheiganikah he is at right in moon. true American indian already he is there yet.

"I heard russia want it to get their befor us. when I was their [there, at Ann Arbor] once I was start telling you about this and we start talking about something else so I didn't finish it. When I was young my good old dad and my uncle use to tell story in the evening. we all love listening story that the time my dad told this story about the brave man and the moon.

Mr. Sheiganikah

it mean some kind of bird

I hope you like the story. hope to hear from again. from your Aunt . . . tell my honey Add Hi.''

Aside from the fascinating implications of her story for the Department of State, the letter tells a great deal about Mountain Wolf Woman. She had set no price on the materials I had ordered and considered my payment more than she would have asked as a fair price. Thus, the story is offered to even the balance, a state of affairs the Winnebago like to maintain. She is also conscious of the importance I place on sources of information and the meaning of words. Her sense of orderliness is shown in her choice of a story to send me. It ties up a loose end of conversation begun during her visit. Finally, instead of merely signing the letter as my aunt, she stresses the relationship to both my husband and me in her final statement.

To Mountain Wolf Woman, aunt, friend and informant, I extend my heartfelt thanks for allowing her autobiography to be published both for its own personal appeal and for the insights it may offer scholarly investigators.

Mountain Wolf Woman

Courtesy The Speltz Studio, Black River Falls, Wisconsin.

Mountain Wolf Woman at about
the time of her first marriage.
Her blouse, jewelry, and
the ribbon-work shawl over
her arm were typical of the
finery she wore to her new home
to be distributed as gifts to her
husband's female relatives.

Mountain Wolf Woman and her husband, Bad Soldier, in 1908.
By the turn of the century Winnebago men dressed in the
fashion of white men, while Winnebago women retained
distinctively Indian styles of dress and adornment as shown.

Mountain Wolf Woman's brother-in-law and classificatory grandfather, who taught her Indian medicines. He was about sixty years old when this picture was taken.

Mountain Wolf Woman's brother, Big Winnebago, alias Crashing Thunder, about 1902. At this time Winnebago men did not ordinarily wear long hair, but Big Winnebago discovered that flowing locks were an asset in finding work as a performer in the so-called Wild West shows.

Mountain Wolf Woman's sister, Fourth Daughter, as a young woman. This is the sister who reared Mountain Wolf Woman's two oldest children.

Mountain Wolf Woman's oldest brother, the true Crashing Thunder, about 1900.

Courtesy Bureau of American Ethnology, Smithsonian Institution.

Three Winnebago girls dressed in all their finery to have their picture taken, about 1900. Mountain Wolf Woman was dressed in this fashion at the time of her first marriage, when she went to live at her husband's home. The brooches, rings, bracelets, and earrings were made by the Winnebago from silver or German-silver.

Winnebago mother and son dressed in exceptionally fine and complete examples of the type of clothing and adornment which developed during the fur trade period of the eighteenth and early nineteenth centuries. Moccasins and leggings were made of deerskin, but other materials were obtained in trade from whites and adapted to Winnebago tastes. By 1900, about the time this picture was taken, such costumes were worn only for ceremonial and festive occasions, such as a visit to the photographer.

White spectators watching Winnebago ladies'
Sunday afternoon poker game near
Black River Falls, about 1910.

A Medicine Dance lodge. Woman on the ground at the
left has been ritually "shot."

Courtesy Milwaukee Public Museum.

Winnebago Indians picking cranberries near
Black River Falls, about 1905.

Winnebago wigwam about 1900, covered with sheets of elm
bark and roofed with strips of cattail matting as well
as canvas. The slab of wood against the curtained entrance
indicated that the family was not home, thus visitors
would not enter.

Scene at old Winnebago cemetery near Black River Falls,
1960. Structures of the type on the right are still
occasionally erected over new graves, where food is placed
for the spirit of the deceased. When scoffing whites
inquire how the dead person is going to come
and eat his food, the Winnebago have a ready reply,
"The same way dead white people smell their flowers!"

Courtesy The Speltz Studios, Black River Falls, Wisconsin.

Winnebago Indians on the main street of Black River Falls
probably congregated while waiting for payment
of annuity money from their treaties. The picture
was taken prior to 1911, as shown by the wooden
sidewalks which were replaced with cement ones in that year.

🌿 CONTENTS

CHAPTER I

❧ EARLIEST RECOLLECTIONS

Mother said she had me at our grandfather's home,—at East
Fork River. We lived there in the spring, April, at the time
they were making maple sugar.[1] She said that after a while
the weather became pleasant, everything was nice and green,
and we moved from this place back to where we usually lived,
—at Levis Creek, near Black River Falls. There father built
a log house. I suppose it took a long time to build it because
mother said the log house was newly finished when I walked
there for the first time. There, where we regularly lived,
mother and father planted their garden.

In the summer that followed the second spring,—after my
first birthday, we went to Black River Falls. Mother, oldest
sister White Thunder and I went to town. We were returning
and mother carried me on her back. I was restless and she had
taken me off the cradleboard. I remember being there on
mother's back. We crossed a creek and I saw the water swirl-
ing swiftly. Mother said, "Ahead is your older sister." A
woman was walking in front of us carrying an empty cradleboard. I saw that she held up her skirt just high enough
to wade through the water. After that I forgot. Once I asked
mother if that ever happened. I told her what I had seen.
"Oh," mother said, "I remember, that was your oldest sister
White Thunder who carried your empty cradle on her back.—
Do you remember that?" "Yes," I said. "You were probably

1

frightened," she said, "and perhaps that is why you remember." [2]

White Thunder was the oldest child in our family and Crashing Thunder was second. Then followed second older sister, Wíhaŋga * Bald Eagle. Next was Hénaga, the second son; he was called Strikes Standing. Then came the third son, Hágaga,[3] and he was called Big Winnebago, Hakśigaga, the third daughter died when she was still quite small. They did not know how this death came about. However, there was an old lady who was related to my mother, and any time that my father brought home deer from hunting, summer, winter, anytime my father killed deer, this old lady got some. Yet, the old lady was envious of my mother about her share of the meat. Mother used to say that she poisoned Hakśigaga. She killed her because of jealousy about meat.[4] Next was the fourth daughter, Hinákega. She was called Distant Flashes Standing. And then I was the last child.—"Poor quality" they used to say of that one.

It was about the time that my older sister Bald Eagle was born that they went to Nebraska.[5] Mother used to say they were taken to Nebraska that winter; they were moved from one land to another. Many Winnebago were moved to Nebraska and there mother took her three children. Grandmother had relatives in Nebraska. Grandmother was the oldest daughter in her family. In Nebraska she saw her sisters, the second and third daughters. They were very eager to see their relatives. But, mother said, some of the Wisconsin Winnebago did not like the removal. Some even cried because they were taken there. However, mother used to say, "The fact that we would see my relatives made me happy that we were going. And when we reached the Missouri River, our uncles came to meet us. When they heard we were coming, Squeaking

* See Appendix C for Pronunciation Guide.

Wing and Captures The Lodge and a third uncle Hágaga came to meet us."[6]

As their uncle Squeaking Wing came through the train he called out, "Bends The Boughs, where is she? Bends The Boughs, where is she?"[7] At last he found them and there was much rejoicing when they saw one another. Brother Crashing Thunder was dressed in a fringed buckskin outfit, and when my uncles saw him they lifted him up in the air and they said, "Oh, how cute our nephew is!" Eventually they arrived at the reservation.

It was winter. Everyone had his own camping outfit, and they all made their homes here and there. They built wigwams. Then spring came and mother said that the Winnebago died in great numbers. Deaths occurred almost every day. When someone died, the Winnebago carried away their dead, crying as they walked. All those who had a death in the family cried as they walked along. They were going to the graveyard, and there was much weeping.

Mother was frightened. "Why do we stay here?" she said. "I am afraid because the people are all dying. Why do we not go back home?" They were with some uncles at the time. The first was called Good Village, the next was called Big Náqiga and the third was called Little Náqiga.[8] In the spring they moved to the Missouri River where they cut down some big willow trees and made dugout canoes big enough for two, mother said. She must have been talking about fairly big boats that they made. There in the spring when the weather is very pleasant, mother used to say, a large group went down the Missouri River. Thus she returned home with some of her relatives. They went down the Missouri to River's Mouth Place as they used to call St. Louis. From there they travelled back on the Mississippi River, they travelled upstream on the Mississippi.

3

Eventually they stopped at a certain place where they saw some white people. Nobody knew how to speak English, so they said, "Where is Hénaga? Where is Hénaga? He is the only one who knows the name of that place." They meant Captures The Lodge, who was just a little boy. When they brought him they said to him, "Say it! Say it!" He was the only one who knew that one word, and he said, "Prarsheen? Prarsheen?" I guess he was saying "Prairie du Chien." Then the white people understood him,—and said it was Prairie du Chien. They stopped there for a while and eventually they left and arrived at La Crosse. They lived there for a time and then they moved out towards Black River Falls.

It seems that many Winnebago came back to Wisconsin. My family were evidently not the only ones who returned. Also, some of the Winnebago in Wisconsin lived way out in the country a great distance from any town. These people said that they had not been found so they did not go to Nebraska, mother said. Thus, not all of the Winnebago left in the removal.

It must have been at this time that my parents took up land, that is, a homestead. Some of them acquired homesteads there at Black River Falls.[9] However, father was not interested in such things. Even when they were in Nebraska his brother said, "Register, older brother, claim some land for yourself and claim some for your children." But father did not do it, so they did not have any land in Nebraska. Mother and her uncles did not take any land, but some of the Winnebago took land in Nebraska so they had property, but eventually they sold it.[10] However, my parents did not realize what they were doing and that is why they acted as they did. Some of the Indians took homesteads but father did not understand so he did not take a homestead. That was when my mother took a homestead. There was an old man who was a grandfather to us who took land. His name was Many Trails. I used to see him; he was a little old man. He said to my mother, ''Granddaughter, why do you not claim some land? I claimed some and if you take a homestead right next to me, then we can live beside each other.'' So mother took forty acres.

Indians did not look ahead to affairs of this sort. They never looked to the future. They only looked to the present insofar as they had enough to sustain themselves. This is the way the Indians used to live. The fact that my father did not care to obtain any land was because he was a member of the Thunder Clan. ''I do not belong to the Earth,'' he said, ''I do not belong to the Earth and I have no concern with land.'' This is why he was not interested in having any land.[11] But mother was also one,—one of the bird clan people; she belonged to the Eagle Clan.[12] She said, ''By this means we will have some place to live,'' and so she took forty acres. Here my father built the log house where we usually lived.

Once when I recalled that we camped at a place where the country was very beautiful, Mother said, ''You were then about two years old.'' I remember there was a fish there. That beautiful country where we were camping was at Black River Falls at the old depot in back of what is now G.W.'s general store. There was not a house around. We lived there in the spring of the year and my father fished. I suppose all of the Indians fished. There my father speared a big fish, an enormous fish, a sturgeon. When my father brought it home, carrying it over his shoulder, the tail dragged on the ground. He brought it back to where we were living. There I saw this big fish that looked like a man with a big fat belly, lying on his side with his belly protruding. I remembered that and then I forgot.

We must have been camped at the Black River where the

5

bank is very steep. There they lost me and everybody helped
my mother look for me.—They were afraid I fell in the water
there, over that high bank. There was an old lady and my
mother brought her tobacco. Anything they asked of her, the
old lady always knew the answer. They brought her tobacco
because she was able to do this.[13] Before she was able to say
anything, somebody came back from town. They all said,
"Sigax̣unuga is lost! Sigax̣unuga is lost!" Then the person
who returned from town said, "Oh, her father is in town with
his daughter, leading her by the hand."—It seems that father
was going toward town. On the way there was a cow which
was probably tethered there and I was frightened by that cow.
Father did not know that I was following along behind him.
Evidently, in fear of that cow, I began to cry. Then father
led me by the hand. He went to town taking me with him. In
time we returned, and so they brought me back alive—.

We probably went back to our home again that spring as it
must have been at that time that I was sick. I was very sick
and my mother wanted me to live. She hoped that I would not
die, but she did not know what to do. At that place there was
an old lady whose name was Wolf Woman and mother had
them bring her. Mother took me and let the old lady hold me.
"I want my little girl to live," mother said, "I give her to
you. Whatever way you can make her live, she will be yours."
That is where they gave me away.[14] That old lady wept.
"You have made me think of myself. You gave me this dear
little child. You have indeed made me think of myself. Let it
be thus. My life, let her use it. My grandchild, let her use my
existence. I will give my name to my own child. The name
that I am going to give her is a holy name. She will reach an
old age." There they named me with a Wolf Clan name;
Xehaćiwiŋga they called me.[15]—It means to make a home in

a bluff or a mountain, as the wolf does, but in English I just say my name is Mountain Wolf Woman.

I do not know if they were jealous of me and that is why they never called me by that name. Just once in a while they called me by that name.[16]

CHAPTER II

✿ LIVELIHOOD

In March we usually travelled to the Mississippi River close to La Crosse,[1] sometimes even across the river, and then we returned again in the last part of May. We used to live at a place on the edge of the Mississippi called Caved In Breast's Grave. My father, brother-in-law and brothers used to trap there for muskrats. When they killed the muskrats my mother used to save the bodies and hang them up there in great numbers. When there were a lot of muskrats then they used to roast them on a rack. They prepared a lot of wood and built a big fire. They stuck four crotched posts into the ground around the fire and placed poles across the crotches. Then they removed the burning wood and left the embers. They put a lot of fine wood crisscross and very dense on the frame. On this the muskrats were roasted, placed all above the fireplace. As the muskrats began roasting, the grease dripped off nice and brown and then the women used long pointed sticks to turn them over and over. The muskrat meat made a lot of noise as it cooked. When these were cooked, the women put them aside and placed some more on the rack. They cooked a great amount of muskrats.—When they were cooled, the women packed them together and stored them for summer use.

In the spring when my father went trapping on the Mississippi and the weather became very pleasant my sister once said, "It is here that they dig yellow water lily roots." So, we all went out, my mother and sisters and everybody. When we got to a slough where the water lilies were very dense, they took off their shoes, put on old dresses and went wading into the water. They used their feet to hunt for the roots. They dug them out with their feet and then the roots floated up to the surface. Eventually, my second oldest sister happened upon one. My sister took one of the floating roots, wrapped it about with the edge of her blouse and tucked it into her belt. I thought she did this because it was the usual thing to do. I saw her doing this and when I happened upon a root I took it and did the same thing. I put it in my belt too. And then everybody laughed at me! "Oh, Little Siga is doing something! She has a water lily root in her belt!" Everybody laughed at me and yelled at me. My sister had done that because she was pregnant. I suppose she did that to ward off something because she was pregnant. Thus she would not affect the baby and would have good luck finding the roots.[2] Because I saw her do that, I did the same thing, and so they teased me.

When they dug up a lot of roots in this fashion they put them in a gunny sack, filling it half full and even more. Then we carried them back to camp and my mother and all my sisters scraped them. The roots have an outside covering and they scraped that off and sliced them.—They look something like a banana. The women then strung the slices and hung them up to dry in order to store them. They dried a great amount, flour sacks full. During the summer they sometimes cooked them with meat and they were really delicious.

Upon returning home, mother and father planted a garden in front of the log house where we usually lived. Nearby stood the well that my father had made. When people leaned over the edge to peer in they could just barely see the water shimmering at the bottom.[3] There were four posts going all the way down to the bottom and these were nailed about with boards which lined the length of the shaft and extended above the ground around the well. A shelf was built around the top of the well and over this was a little house which contained a pulley wheel. To this a bucket was attached by a long rope. It was a long cylindrical bucket with a hole and stopper on the bottom. This they sent down to the water. When the filled bucket was pulled up, it was rested on the shelf that went around the well and this released the stopper so the water ran out. The water was icy cold. The Indians used to come there for water. It was very good water that we had.

At the time we were there when mother and father planted a garden, the blueberries ripened and we picked blueberries. There were pine trees all around where we lived, the kind of pine trees that are very tall and look as if they had been trimmed all up the trunk almost to the top. That is the way it used to be around our home. The pine trees were very dense and there was no underbrush.[4] Under the trees the blueberries grew in profusion. All the Indians picked blueberries. They came carrying boxes on their backs and when they filled the boxes they left. At that time they used to come to our house for water, and when they brought the water up, the turning wheel would say, ''gink, gink, gink, gink.''

All the berry pickers carried boxes on their backs. The boxes were square and were divided into four square compartments. There were two holes on opposite sides of the box and cords were strung across these holes. They called these boxes waŋkšíkwak 'ʔín, that is, carry on a person's back. They used to carry them by horseback too, a pair slung in front and in back of the person riding the horse. This is the way they went to town to sell the berries. There they bought food for themselves, bringing the berry boxes back full of groceries. This is the way that they earned money.

They were paid a good price; fifty cents a quart is the price they used to get toward the beginning of the season, and as the season wore on, toward the end, they got a quarter. They saved their money and they even bought horses. Some of the Indians had no wagons and that is why they let the horses carry the berries, but some of them had wagons. Thus the Indians came through history.[5] That is the way they procured food for themselves. They saved food and they saved money.

When various foods were ripe the people dried them. They also steamed things underground. They harvested a lot of corn and carried it home on their backs. When I was a little girl our family was large. I was the youngest and I had three older brothers and two older sisters. Another older sister and I were the younger ones. When they harvested the gardens, they harvested a great amount. They steamed the corn. In the evening they dug a pit and heated stones there in a big fire. They put the stones in the pit and when the stones became red hot they took out all the wood and embers and put in the corn husks. Then they put in the fully ripe corn and covered it with more husks. Finally they covered it with the earth that had been dug out. They covered the pit but they left four holes in which they poured water. We used to hear the red hot stones make a rumbling sound.

Then, very early in the morning they opened the pit with great care. They removed the earth very carefully and finally when they reached the husks they took them out. Eventually they reached the corn and it was thoroughly cooked. It was really hot! They took the corn out and put it on the husks. Sometimes other people heard about it and worked with my family. The helpers came and spread out a big piece of canvas on which they put the corn. Then they used metal teaspoons or clam shells to scrape the corn off the cobs. They used to dry it and after it was dried you could see sackfuls of corn standing here and there. They dried the corn in the sun and put it in white flour sacks. Some corn was allowed to remain on the stalks after it was ripe. This they saved for seed. In addition to saving seed they made hominy of this dried corn. They mixed it with ashes and popped it to make hominy.

Squash was also dried. The women pared the squash, cut it in two and sliced it to form rings. They cut down forked trees, peeled them, and strung the squash on poles they laid across the forks. A lot of squash hung on this framework. The Indians generally dried squash in this way and saved it for winter.

They used to dry blueberries too, berries they did not sell. They dried the blueberries and cooked them in the winter time. The blueberries were boiled with dried corn and I used to think this was delicious. That is what we used to eat.

They used to dig a hole to save whatever they were not going to use during the winter. They kept out whatever they thought they would need for that winter and they saved in the hole what they would eat in the spring. Seed was also buried in the ground. They made a hole and buried things in it and took them out as they were required. "Dig up that which is buried," they used to say.

They also dried Indian potatoes.[6] My grandmother and my mother's younger sister and I used to gather them.—Indian potatoes grow wild, where it is wooded with dense hazel bushes, near creeks. The vines of the Indian potatoes are like strings stretched out, a lot of strings extending in all directions. That is the way the vines grow, tangled up around the bushes. The women would try poking here and there with a hoe and then they would hit upon them. The potatoes would be linked to each other as if they were strung together. Then they would dig a lot of them. After they dug them up, they cut up the links and dried them. When they cooked these things they added sugar and boiled them until the water was gone, and then we peeled off the skins. Oh, they were really delicious things!—

Stealing from mice is something I never did but aunt and grandmother told me about it. They would go off in the brush, in the woods, and steal wild beans from the mice. These mice know how to store things. Running back and forth, the mice carried things to a particular place. Their little trails showed the way they went into their little holes in the ground. There they gathered very many of those wild beans. Grandmother said that when a family had a lot of little boys it used to be said of the last born, the youngest one, that he is married to one of these mice. It was that boy who used to find the storehouses. That is why they used to say the little boys married little mice. Mother's brothers were all big and they did not have any little boy. Even my youngest uncle was grown up, but they used to say, "Squeaking Wing's wives have stored some things, let us go look for some of them." They always found some. Grandmother used to say that some women knew very well how to look for wild beans. They would stand some place and look around. "There is one over there!" they used to say, and "There is one right here too!" When they scraped away the leaves and the earth there the holes used to be, just all full of wild beans. They would take them and save them. —Sometimes they said they found a bucketful, I do not know how big a bucket they meant. Those beans were very good; I ate some of them. When I went to Nebraska they gave me some

13

there. I cooked them in the same way I cook any beans. The beans that we eat today are good, but wild beans are much more delicious.[7]

When I was small the Winnebago generally went to pick cranberries after they were through taking care of their gardens.[8] We used to do that too. When we arrived at the marsh there were many Indians who camped together there and picked cranberries. The men used rakes and the women picked by hand. As the women were picking and they reached the edge of the ditch, they all sat on the edge of the ditch in a long row, side by side.[9] They picked ahead of themselves in a straight line, a bushel-sized box at each woman's side. They would put aside as many boxes as they thought they would fill so they would not run out of boxes. They left their boxes as they filled them, and if you looked down a line you could see the row of filled boxes. As they filled each box they took along another empty box. At noon they went back to the camp to eat.[10] Some people even brought their lunches along and ate there at the marsh. I used to think it was great fun when we took food and ate outside.

That is what people did in the fall. They were making money to save. When they finished there they went deer hunting. They were trying to earn money for themselves and they probably earned quite a bit but I did not know what they were earning.[11] The women used to pick into a big dishpan and when it was full it was emptied into the box. We children used to pick too. We used small pails. Wherever mother sat, I used to sit next to her and I would pick cranberries. When I filled the pail I emptied it into mother's bushel box. My sister did the same thing on the other side of mother. That is what I used to do.

When we were there a peddler of general merchandise often came around. When he said the word for a white man's shirt, he would say, "šorot." He was a white man with black hair and black mustache and he did not know how to speak English.[12] When this peddler came they would all call out, "Oh, šorot is here!" They used to call him šorot.

The Indians were making money and that is why they used to come around and sell things. Somebody came around selling pies. I used to think that was very nice. Mother often bought things from these peddlers and then we used to eat pie. After all, the Indians were using campfires outside and could not bake pies and cakes, and so they had a bakery shop there at the marsh.

That cranberry picking place is gone now. Iron Mountain Marsh they used to call it and I do not even know the English name for it. That cranberry marsh no longer exists because at one time a big forest fire came through there. When the people fled they said that they had to put the old people in the ditches. They could not flee with them in time so they put the old people in the water in the ditches. I believe the marsh ceased to exist at that time. The entire stand of cranberry bushes was burned up.

After cranberry time they went on the fall migration to hunt deer. That is what we always did, we went travelling to hunt deer. At that time my father did not have to buy any deer license. They never used to pay for such things. When they went deer hunting the white people did not spy on them. That is how it used to be at that time. They killed as many deer as they deemed necessary. We used to travel a certain distance east of Neillsville where there used to be a woods. There were not many white people around at that time. That is where we used to go in the fall. That is where we used to live and almost immediately the hunters used to bring in deer. They wrapped the deer in autumn leaves and carried the deer on their backs. As they were approaching you could see the red leaves moving along here and there, as they came home with the freshly killed deer. Just as soon as we arrived, the first day, they always brought home game. It was always this way. Sometimes they even used to bring in a bear.

Four or five households of Indians migrated to this area where they built long wigwams; my father and my brothers, also my brother-in-law Cloud, and another brother-in-law Little Náqiga as well as their relatives, and sometimes our uncles came there too. Our family was large enough to require a two-fireplace wigwam. We lived in a rush wigwam. My grandmother and my mother made our house of cattail matting. The wigwam was covered with mats of cattail stalks. The inside of the house was never smoky. I suppose that was because it was properly made.[13] It was very pleasant to live in a rush wigwam. My older sister White Thunder and my brother-in-law Cloud lived next door, but they lived in a large round wigwam. Another person who lived in a big round wigwam was Cloud's brother who was called Big Thunder. Big Thunder's wife's name was Axjiŋwiŋga—and I do not know what that would mean in English. Her mother's name was Four Women and her husband's name was Daylight.

One time when we had been living there only a short time, as I recall, this old man, Daylight, died. When he was about to die he was very sick. He was really very sick but he said that he wanted to see the daylight, he wanted to go outside. He said this as he lay there. Upon hearing this my mother came home. She had evidently gone to visit him. She said, "My sons, he is to be pitied that he is saying this. Go and carry him. Take him outside. Let him see the daylight." So, my older brothers did as they were told to do. Then the old man said as he lay there, "Daylight, at one time I knew this daylight well. That accounts for my name; they called me Daylight. But nothing can be done to help me, so I am going away. At one time there was a certain food of which I was fond, skunk meat. If you should kill a skunk, cook it and think of me as you do so. Think of me and scatter some tobacco for me. Whatever you want when you do this, it will be granted to you.'' That is what the old man said. That is the way the old people were; the old people were supposed to be respected. ''Respect those old people,'' mother and father used to say to us. That is what we used to do. We respected the old people, but today they do not respect the old people.

CHAPTER III

⚘ GROWING UP

At the place where they hunted, father and older brother killed as many deer as they would need for a feast.[1] They set aside ten deer on a high, narrow rack made for storing meat. They cut down crotched poles and set them up in a rectangle with poles across the crotches and other poles forming a platform, similar to the open-sided square shelters used as sun shades, but narrower and higher.[2] They put the deer on it and covered them with the hides.

Once there was a lot of snow on the ground when we went back home. We had come in wagons and when we went back the wagon wheels made a loud noise rolling over the snow. We always returned to our home at Black River Falls where we ordinarily lived. Other Winnebago also did this. They too went away some place, wherever they chose to go to hunt, and then they would give a feast. Father and all the Indians used to give feasts. Father used to hold big feasts, ten fireplaces they said. The row of fireplaces used to stretch off into the distance. Many Indians attended and father used to feed a wigwam full of people. There we would dance all night. Sometimes children were named at feasts.[3] This is what they used to do time and again. Sometimes, those who had been fasting would then eat at the feast.

That is what my older brother Hágaga did, he alone fasted. Hénaga did not have any patience with such things, but

WINNEBAGO LANDS, CESSIONS, AND RESERVATIONS

The Winnebago Indians ceded their homeland in Wisconsin and northern Illinois by treaties in 1829, 1832, and 1837. Between 1846 and 1865 they were prevailed upon by the government to exchange one reservation for another until they were finally settled upon their present reservation in northeastern Nebraska. This reservation, about 100,000 acres, was reduced by about two-thirds after 1888, when the Indians were granted patents in fee to individual allotments and could enter into private sales. The questionable practices involved in purchases of Indian lands throughout the nation caused the government to enforce stricter regulations on land sales in 1934. About half of the tribe is presently enrolled on the Nebraska reservation. However, a portion of the tribe claimed that the treaty of 1837 had been fraudulent and therefore refused to be removed from Wisconsin. The last forcible removal of the Wisconsin Winnebago occurred in 1874 and figures in Mountain Wolf Woman's story. After 1875 the Winnebago who wished to remain in Wisconsin were permitted to take up forty-acre homesteads on the public domain, and Mountain Wolf Woman's mother was among those who took up land in Wisconsin. At present, over 1,500 Winnebago make their home in their original tribal territory.

Charles Royce and Cyrus Thomas. "Indian Land Cessions," *18th Annual Report, Bureau of American Ethnology, Smithsonian Institution*, 1896–97, Part II. Official Files, Office of Land Clerk, Winnebago Agency, Winnebago, Nebraska, 1950.

brother Hágaga fasted in the woods. My father built a shelter
for them to live in and they slept there four nights. But my
older brother Hénaga did not do that. Hénaga came home
during that time. Mother wept. "Why did you do that? Why
did you do that?" she said. "Oh," he said, "I am sick of it
so I stopped." But brother Hágaga stayed there. He was trying to remain until feast time.[4] When it was about time for
the feast, father and his nephews built the lodge and made
all the preparations for it. All these kinsmen that father would
invite to the feast he could make work for him.[5] That is what
they did. Brother was allowed to return at the time of the
feast since at that time one who fasts for a vision may eat.

When he was about to return they went around the lodge
with a deer hide. They took a deer hide around the morning
he was going to come back. Brother Hágaga must have been
a little boy at the time they were taking this white deer hide
around. They used it when dancing, taking the deer hide and
dancing with it. It seemed to be a very pleasant time. There
brother cried to the Thunders. Our aunts and older sisters
heard my older brother crying and they cried too, they said.
Today they do not do that any more.[6]

My older sister Hinakega and I also used to fast. They used
to make us do this. We would blacken our cheeks and would
not eat all day. That was at the time of the hunting I have
told about, before we returned from hunting. We used to
blacken our cheeks with charcoal at the time father left in
the morning to go hunting. We used coals from the fire to
blacken our cheeks and we did not eat all day.[7] I used to play
outside but my older sister used to sit indoors and weave
yarn belts. When father returned from hunting in the evening
he used to say to us, "Go cry to the Thunders." When father
was ready to eat he would give us tobacco and say to us,
"Here, go cry to the Thunders." Just as it was getting dark

my sister and I used to go off a certain distance and she would
say to me, "Go stand by a tree and I am going to go farther
on." We used to stand there and look at the stars and cry
to the Thunders. This is what we used to sing:

"Oh, Good Spirits
Will they pity me? Here am I, pleading."

We used to sing and scatter tobacco, standing there and
watching the stars and the moon. We used to cry because,
after all, we were hungry. We used to think we were pitied.[8]
We really wanted to mean what we were saying.

When we finished with our song we scattered tobacco at
the foot of the tree and returned home. When we got back
home father ate and we ate too. We did not eat all day, only
at night, and when we had finished eating we put the dishes
away. Then father used to say, "All right, prepare your
bedding and go to bed and I will tell you some stories."
I really enjoyed listening to my father tell stories. Everybody, the entire household, was very quiet and in this
atmosphere my father used to tell stories. He used to tell
myths, the sacred stories, and that is why I also know some
myths. I do not know all of them any more, I just remember
parts of stories.

Again we went hunting and returned to Black River Falls
and had our feast there. I was a little girl. The people followed
the same cycle, winter, spring, summer, and when it was almost fall my oldest brother said, "My little sister should go
to school." I was nine years old. He said, "I like to hear
women speak English so I would like my little sister to learn
how to speak English." They let me go to school at Tomah,
Wisconsin, and I attended school there for two years.[9] Then I
did not go to school again for a long time. Well, whatever the
reason, that is the way with Indians. The Indians do not stay

home so that their children can attend school. That is what they have done through the years, but at present they can no longer act in this way.

Then I lived at home and the family went on a short hunting trip. After that they went off to find cranberries and on our return we stopped at the home of grandfather Náqi-Johnga. There it was that mother told me how it is with little girls when they become women. "Some time," she said, "that is going to happen to you. From about the age of thirteen years this happens to girls. When that happens to you, run to the woods and hide some place. You should not look at any one, not even a glance. If you look at a man you will contaminate his blood. Even a glance will cause you to be an evil person. When women are in that condition they are unclean." Once, after our return to grandfather's house, I was in that condition when I awoke in the morning.

Because mother had told me to do so, I ran quite far into the woods where there were some bushes. The snow was still on the ground and the trees were just beginning to bud. In the woods there was a broken tree and I sat down under this fallen tree. I bowed my head with my blanket wrapped over me and there I was, crying and crying. Since they had forbidden me to look around, I sat there with my blanket over my head. I cried. Then, suddenly I heard the sound of voices. My sister Hiñakega and my sister-in-law found me. Because I had not come back in the house, they had looked for me. They saw my tracks in the snow, and by my tracks they saw that I ran. They trailed me and found me. "Stay here," they said. "We will go and make a shelter for you," and they went home again. Near the water's edge of a big creek, at the rapids of East Fork River, they built a little wigwam. They covered it with canvas. They built a fire and put straw there for me, and then they came to get me. There I sat in the little wigwam. I was crying. It was far, about a quarter of a mile from home. I was crying and I was frightened. Four times they made me sleep there.[10] I never ate. There they made me fast. That is what they made me do. After the third time that I slept, I dreamed.

There was a big clearing. I came upon it, a big, wide open field, and I think there was a rise of land there. Somewhat below this rise was the big clearing. There, in the wide meadow, there were all kinds of horses, all colors. I must have been one who dreamed about horses. I believe that is why they always used to give me horses.[11]

Spring arrived, and again deer hunting time, and winter back at Black River Falls when my father gave feasts, and then it was spring again. Once more we moved to the Mississippi River.[12] When the muskrat season was over we returned to our home. The people engaged in their usual activities, but that time when we returned, after a while, mother and father said that they were not going to put in any garden.—Father must have had word from his uncles, although I did not hear about it. Father's uncles at Wittenberg, Wisconsin, were old men. They lived there at Wittenberg for many years. Father pitied his uncles because they were old and could not help themselves. My parents said that was where we were going to move. My older sister also accompanied us and we moved there. We used big wagons drawn by horses.

North of the town of Marshfield there was a settlement of Indians and we slept there. Some lived in frame houses and some lived in bark-sided gabled cabins with earth-covered roofs. They built these cabins themselves and these were scattered throughout the settlement.[13] They were Potawatomi Indians and mother had relatives there. They were called Chippewa Woman and Hínuga, her daughter. They spoke Winnebago very fluently. Mother knew them and knew that they were living there so we stopped at that place. We must have slept there twice in order to rest the horses. There was a tall frame house where we stayed and the name of the person who lived there was Crotched Tree. He had a wife. It would seem that father was also part Potawatomi because she was his relative. They invited us to eat and so we ate. At that place there was a dance area. It was a sacred place. They invited us to eat there that evening and so we went there to eat.

The wife of Crotched Tree was my father's sister.[14] They gave my parents maple sugar in a hand-woven bag, cakes of hardened syrup which are stored in such bags.[15] In the morning when my mother and father went out I went along. Mother took some things with her when we went to visit the Potawatomi aunt who was my father's sister. Mother brought that woman some necklaces and bracelets and long earrings with coins on the ends. She was very pleased. She was a fine-looking woman. If these people were still living they would be my in-laws because Crotched Tree had daughters of marriageable age and one of them had a son who was the father of my son-in-law. One of my sons-in-law is my nephew.[16]

We left that place and arrived at Wittenberg. We had a grandfather there whose name was High Snake and he lived in a big log cabin. We stopped there and my father went off to get those two dear little old men. They were very old men. It was their son [17] who lived at the place where we stopped. The old men lived at another place and my father went there for them. One was called Good Snake and the other was called Fear The Snake Den. He soon brought them and they began to make preparations at grandfather High Snake's place. They cut trees for lodge poles and hauled them back in a big horse-drawn wagon. There they set up a long lodge. They built a medicine lodge. On the east side where the sun rises they completed it and sang upon reaching that end. My older sister

White Thunder and my older brother Hénaga were initiated into the lodge and I imagine that is why we went there. Evidently father's uncles told us to come there, and because they were old men we went there.

They had the paraphernalia for a medicine dance so the medicine dance was held there. They held the medicine dance as soon as we arrived. During that time Indians came there to Wittenberg from various places. The Indians were real Indians! [18] Some of them brought wagons and some of them let the horses back-pack their belongings. Some of them arrived riding horseback. There were many Indians and they held a medicine dance. We were gathered there in a big group.

When they finished the medicine dance somebody said, "About this time they usually peel and dry slippery elm." They used to tie it in a bundle and white people bought it. They paid a good price for slippery elm. "All right," father said, "we can do that. We are a big family and thus we will be able to eat." That is what they did. Mother and her young ones put up a tent next to my grandfather's home and we lived there. Those who were strong went away some place with a wagon and some household goods. Where the trees were very dense they stopped and they asked for the slippery elm from the white people who owned the woods. They called it slippery elm; it is something like the elm tree. They asked, "Could you not give that kind to us so that we can make something to sell?" The white people said, "Help yourself, do whatever it is that you are talking about."

Then they walked about and looked at the trees and wherever they saw a slippery elm they skinned it. They cut the bark from the base of the tree and pulled it loose up to the very top of the tree. Then they slashed it off and it fell down like folding cloth. The trees were easily peeled. Even one tree produced a lot of bark. They measured the bark with their arms and cut it to that length. They made piles big enough for a person to carry on his back and when they had a load for everyone they started back to wherever they were camping. The women peeled off the outer bark with jack-knives. They made drying racks and hung up all the bark. They dried a lot of bark and tied it in bundles. In a short time they made many bundles. Only the drying took a long time. They took the bundles to some town where the white people bought slippery elm.[19] They used to come and visit those of us who were living at home and bring us food. Then they went away again to the big forest where they travelled about gathering slippery elm. Today they no longer do that. Today the white people who have timber land keep it for themselves. Years ago it was not that way and the white people used to say, ''Help yourself, do whatever it is that you are talking about.'' They looked for slippery elm and they prepared it to sell. Whatever the situation they always found something to do and were able to obtain food for themselves by such methods. Whatever the circumstances, the Indian is always doing something useful.

It must have been fall by that time and my sisters went back to Black River Falls. Father, mother, my brothers and my older sister Hiñakega did not go back. We remained there for a while. One of my grandfathers who was called Rattle-snake had land next to the highway and told us that we should live there. My father made a big round wigwam of bark and there we lived. That fall I did not go to school at all. We moved to another place where my father trapped. He was still with my grandfathers. We went to a place where there is a lake, Green Lake it is called. My grandfathers were acquainted with some white people where they used to trap. Father trapped there along with the grandfathers and they went to some other places as well. That was during the fall and when the cold weather was about to set in we went back to Wittenberg. They should have put me in school that fall. Not until we returned did they put me in school. I went to the Lutheran Mission School at Wittenberg. I had attended school at Tomah and finally I went to school again. I was a teen-age girl and I went to school there every year.

Once, my older brothers and some other people were going to go some place to dance. I think it was at Chicago.[20] One time they sent me a bicycle. Oh, I was proud. Nobody had a bicycle. I was the first one to have a bicycle, a girl's bicycle. My brothers did that for me. The girls really thought something of me. They coaxed me to ride my bicycle and they pampered me. Bicycles were rare at that time. I suppose I was the first of the students to have a bicycle.

At the school there was an Oneida woman who was the girls' matron. She was called Nancy Smith. Whenever the Indians were going to have a dance, Nancy Smith and I would ride there on our bicycles. Once when the Indians were going to hold a dance Nancy said, "It would be more fun if we went by horseback." In town they used to have ponies at the place where they sold wagons. They used to be tough. She asked me to hire some of those ponies. There were many horse stalls at the livery stable where I went for the ponies. They put saddles on the horses and I sat on one and went outside. I had a terribly hard time getting on as it was skittish. Leading the other one, I started back. The horse I was riding tried to run, but I held back on the reins. I had to fight that horse all the way, but I finally got back. I used to think horseback riding was a lot of fun. I was like a boy riding horses. When I got back, Nancy also had a hard time getting in the saddle. We started off immediately, letting the horses run. After a while we held the reins in on the horses so they would walk.

We continued on our way letting the horses alternately run and walk. We finally arrived where the Indians were dancing. We dismounted and sat and watched the people dance. We sat on a big log, watching them dance. The horses were standing nearby and we were sitting there holding the reins. They had been having a war dance and then they had a "squaw dance."[21] Four Women came over and asked me to dance. Nancy told me to go ahead and dance, and so I did. I was dressed in "citizens clothing,"[22] and I really danced! When they used to ask me to dance I would do so. They said that they really liked it for me. When I watched the horse races they used to tell me that they liked it when I enjoyed myself dancing.[23] Whenever something of that sort was taking place I was never embarrassed, no matter the circumstances. I always used to be there. Eventually we started back. We arrived at town and returned the horses. I do not know how much Nancy paid for their hire. When we got to town we walked back to the school.

Nancy Smith was the girls' matron in charge of sewing. Later she was put in charge of the bakery. Whatever she did, she always called upon me to be with her. Eventually she married a workman there at the school.

CHAPTER IV

MARRIAGE

Then I stopped attending school. They took me out of school. Alas, I was enjoying school so much, and they made me stop. They took me back home. They had let me go to school and now they made me quit. It was then that they told me I was going to be married. I cried but it did not do any good. What would my crying avail me? They had already arranged it. As they were telling me about it my mother said, "My little daughter, I prize you highly. You alone are the youngest child. I prize you highly but nothing can be done about this matter. It is your brothers' doing. You must do whatever your brothers say. If you do not do so, you are going to embarrass them. They have been drinking again, but if you do not do this they will be disgraced. They might even experience something unfortunate." [1] Thus mother spoke to me. She rather frightened me.

My father said, "My little daughter, you do not have very many things to wear, but you will go riding on your little pony. You do not have anything, but you will not walk there." [2] I had a little horse, a dapple gray kind of pony that was about three years old. Father brought it for me and there the pony stood. They dressed me. I wore a ribbon embroidery skirt and I wore one as a shawl. I wore a heavily beaded binding for the braid of hair down my back, and I had on earrings. It looked as if I were going to a dance. That man was sitting nearby. He started out leading the pony and I followed after. When we reached a road that had high banks on the side he mounted the horse and I got on behind him. That is the way he brought me home. We rode together. That is how I became a daughter-in-law.

As a daughter-in-law I arrived. When I arrived he had me go in the wigwam and I went in and sat down. They told me to sit on the bed and I sat there. I took off all the clothing that I was wearing when I got there. I took it all off. I laid down a shawl and whatever I had, all the finery, I put on it; beads, the necklaces, clothing, even the blouse that I was wearing. Finally, the man's mother came in. Outside the wigwam there were canvas-covered wigwams standing here and there. The woman took the things and left. There were women sitting all about outside. They were his female relatives. They divided the things among themselves. As they distributed the things around, everybody contributed something in return. Two or three days from the time of my arrival they took me back with four horses and a double shawl so full of things they could barely tie the corners together. They took me home and later I received two more horses, so they gave me six horses in all.[3] That is how they used to arrange things for young women in the past. They made the girls marry into whatever family they decided upon. They made the arrangements. That is the way they used to do.

At the time that my mother was combing my hair and I was weeping at the prospect of becoming a daughter-in-law she told me, "Daughter, I prize you very much, but this matter cannot be helped. When you are older and know better, you can marry whomever you yourself think that you want to marry." Mother said that to me and I did not forget it!

In the first place, before they made me get married, my older brother had been drinking and was asleep. I guess he slept there all day and when he awoke that man they made me marry, who was not a drinker, was there. He sat there using his hat to fan away the mosquitoes from my brother's face. That is why they made me marry that man. My brother awoke and he surmised, "He is doing this for me because I have sisters. That is what he is thinking to himself." So they made me marry that man. That is what the Indians used to do in the past.[4]

That man was very easily aroused to jealousy of other men. He used to accuse me of being with other men. That made me angry. I hated him. He used to watch me too. So, I said to him one time, "No matter how closely you watch me, if I am going to leave you, I am going to leave you! There are a lot of things right now that I do not like." That is what I did to him. I left him taking the two children with me.[5]

Before that, however, when Hínuga, my oldest daughter, was a little girl, mother and father were going to hold a medicine dance. My older brother Hénaga the second son, had died after he joined the medicine lodge and they were going to give a medicine dance for him.[6] They were saying that I was to take his place, but I did not even know about it. Likewise, the family that I was living with also asked my father and mother whether they could have me join the lodge. My mother-in-law's mother had been a prominent woman in the medicine lodge and they were going to do this for her. They asked my mother and father if they would let me join the lodge. They said that they asked for me and that mother said, "They are saying something good." Mother said, "She is going to earn something for herself. She is going to earn the right to be a lodge member. They are talking about something which is good." So they told them they approved. Thus, I was initiated into the lodge.

My mother-in-law had a big otterskin medicine bag she

prized highly. She would give it to whomever she wanted to have it, and if I were there she would give it to me. That is what she said to mother. That was to be mine she told her.

Then the time for the medicine dance arrived. I did not even know about it when they told me I was going to join the lodge. They even had me sew some things.[7] They made a lodge and it was there that the woman spoke of it to me. They brought everything there and then we ate our evening meal. We ate at the sitting place.[8] She said to me, ''We are all going to sit here. Daughter-in-law, this way is a good way. It is a way of life, they say. Daughter-in-law, this is what I am contemplating. As I was planning to replace my mother I wondered who could do this thing. It is a good way that the people have to live, my little granddaughter,[9] and you are going to earn a good life for yourself.'' This she said to me. As I thought about it, my head felt prickly.[10] They were going to sing medicine songs and they began talking about it. There they made me join the lodge. Then that night when I joined the lodge they held the rehearsal for initiates.

In the morning they went to the woods and when they arrived there they did all the things they still do when they have a medicine dance. They even ''shot'' me. Then that woman asked about for a medicine bag. She did not give me that big otterskin bag they wanted to give me. She was selfish. She asked about for a medicine bag. Then I was dissatisfied. They finished what they were doing and I looked at my husband and he looked at me. I got up and walked out and we were the first ones to come back. She followed us while we were walking back.

''Well, your mother fooled me,'' I said to him. ''Yes, I heard and saw it too. I did not like it either. Whatever you are thinking, I am thinking the same thing. She said the pouch was yours,'' he said. I said, ''Whenever they ask you to use it, do not use it. Say to her, 'If you want to do so, use it, you prize it so highly, you can use it.' " "Yes," he said, "that is what I am going to say. That is just what I think too." We came away from there in disgust.

We returned to our tent that was near the medicine lodge. I washed myself and combed my hair. Those who had gone to the woods returned. That old lady cried and cried. "Daughter-in-law, daughter-in-law, if you would only just do this for us!" That is what she said to me. She asked me very nicely. I thought to myself, "I will do graciously what she asks me to do,[11] but after while I will do what I want to do." That is what I did. I joined the lodge, but not for long.

But that man was jealous. He used to accuse me of having affairs with other men, even my own male relatives. I hated him. Then when my second daughter was an infant I wanted to go to Black River Falls. They said there was going to be a powwow there. We arrived there in a two-seated buggy I had which belonged to my mother and father. I owned a horse but we left my horse behind and used a horse that belonged to his family. We also used the new harness that his parents owned.—Soon after we arrived, father and mother left for Nebraska. Father was sick and they said he might get better if he went there. So they went to Nebraska.[12]

When the powwow was over and the people from Wittenberg were going home, he said, "Well, are we not going to return?" "No," I said to him, "for my part, I am not going back." "Well," he said, "we have to take back the things that we borrowed. We brought a horse of theirs. After all, it belongs to them."

"And you belong to them too," I said. "Take the horse and let him carry the harness on his back and ride him and go home," I told him. "Leave the wagon here for me, it belongs to my mother and father." The people were preparing to leave and the ones from Wittenberg went back. He put the harness on the horse and let them take it home.—That man stayed around for a while but I would not go back so he finally left too.

As for myself, I went to my grandmother. We had our own tent. "Grandmother," I said, "I am going to borrow some things." "All right," she said, "I am caring for the baby." I said to her, "When I come back, we are going to move." My sister was also going to move. I went to the mission [13] to my niece, the wife of Bright Feather. I said to her, "Niece, I came to borrow something." "All right," she said, "what did you come to borrow?" "A one-horse harness and buggy hitch." "All right, wherever they are take them. What am I using them for? They are yours," she said. There was a wagon going back to the powwow ground and I asked the people to carry back the harness and the hitch. I rode back with them too. When we got back, the man with the wagon attached the single hitch to the buggy and took our double harness and hitch. He said, "I will take these back to your niece at the mission because I will be going that way. They can probably use them." That is what he did. The only horse I had was a big one and I let him pull the buggy alone. I packed everything and headed for the home of my older sister. Thus I left that man.[14]

I took grandmother with me and moved to where one of my sisters was living at Black River Falls. She was there at a cranberry marsh where picking was in progress. Grandmother and I arrived there in the one-horse buggy. We stayed there for a while and then I moved again to a different marsh where another older sister lived. We used to pick cranberries there every day. Across the marsh they held sore eye dances and my brothers-in-law were the hosts.[15] We would go dancing.

Once they said that they were going to hold a medicine dance. My older sister said, "Go if you wish to do so. Then

you will be able to set up housekeeping there for the family.''
I took my tent and grandmother and I went there to the town
of Millston. Red Cloud's wife, Little Wíhaŋga she was called,
was to be initiated and I helped initiate her into the lodge.
We arrived and I put up my tent and we stayed there. It was
soon evening, and then night, and immediately the singing
began at the entrance of the lodge. Brother Hágaga drank
a lot and he did not attend. I thought to myself, ''So much
the better if he does not come.'' We had already entered the
lodge and were sitting there when we could hear off in the
distance, ''Oooooooooooooh! Oʔi, Oʔi, Oʔi!'' This war whoop
could be heard coming from the direction of the road. Older
brother was coming! He was well behaved. Although he was
drunk, he was not very drunk. We continued with the medicine dance and he came in the lodge too. He had four men for
his companions.

A man they called They Bring Him sat in the very first
place. They Bring Him was a big medicine man from Wittenberg. ''Oh,'' he said, ''this is even better. I thought we were
going to be a small group. This is good.'' It began to rain.
The top of the lodge was covered with very heavy canvas and
in between the lodge supports the canvas became filled with
water as it rained. The hollows were filled with water because
the canvas did not leak and the weight of the canvas sagged
down the lodge in the center. When they began the singing
for the dancing we got up and danced.—We had to bend way
down as we danced where the roof sagged. There were puddles
here and there. The people left their blankets behind at the
sitting places when they got up to dance. The path around
the inside of the lodge was full of puddles. My older brother
danced really hard, bending way down war dance style. He
danced and splashed mud on the blankets that the people had
left at their sitting places. We thought that was so funny that

my sister-in-law Four Women and I laughed and laughed. As we were dancing, day overtook us.

They customarily go to the woods then, very early in the morning, and so that is what we did. We left and arrived at the woods. Little Wíhaŋga was a large, heavy woman, and as she watched us perform the shooting rite she was supposed to do whatever we did. When they ''shot'' us we fell down and trembled. Eventually, we shot at her. She landed with a thud and said, ''Ooof!'' When she fell she just stayed on the ground. ''Do as they are doing,'' they would say to her, but she was a big woman and she just could not fall properly. She just could not learn.[16] We continued working with her but finally we came back. There we remained all day at the medicine dance.—Next morning we left. Older brother left with his wife and I took down my tent and left with my grandmother.

There was an old lady called White Woman and another woman called Wave who were living at the place where my sister was living. Wave had a small child and had not wanted to go to the medicine dance. When we were getting ready to go to the medicine dance that old lady had told us, ''If you see my nephew Red Horn there, pinch his ear, shake him up, point the direction to him and bring him back.''—Wave was Red Horn's wife, and she was my sister.[17] He was walking around there when we had arrived at the medicine dance. When we were ready to go home he was sitting in the shade beside a house. I then got down from the buggy and did as they had told me to do. I shook him but I did not take him by the ear. ''Go get in the buggy,'' I said to him, ''they said I was supposed to bring you back.''

''Ho!'' he said. He had a little suitcase that he grabbed and he got in the buggy. He drove. I let him drive the buggy. I brought him back and he laughed and laughed. ''Ah, I was having such a good time and then with great cruelty they brought me back!'' Then they all laughed at him.

We stayed there and picked cranberries until the end of the season, and then we moved back to my other older sister's place. There my older brother asked for the use of a horse, and there Four Women gave me some things:[18] a blouse decorated with little silver brooches, a very nice one, and necklaces and a hair ornament and earrings. They gave me much finery and again I became a woman to be envied. I remained single and lived at my sister's place all winter long. Whenever there was a feast that winter my niece Queen Of Thunder and I used to go to the feast, and we used to dance. There they accused me concerning a man. They gossiped at the winter feast. Alas, I was not even looking at any men. The man that they linked me with began writing letters to me. Well, after all, they were accusing him of it.

Then it became spring and in the spring we camped near Black River Falls where my sister was staying. I went to town to get some things and as I was coming back somebody behind me said, ''sister, sister.'' I stopped. It was my oldest brother. ''Sister,'' he said, ''whoever is saying things to you, I would like it if you did as he says. Little sister, your first husband was not any good. You would never have had any place for yourself and at his home you would have always been doing all the work. But this lad who is now talking to you lives alone. He knows how to care for himself. If you make a home someplace, then I will have someplace to go to visit.'' That is what my older brother said to me. I did not say anything. And just standing right there was that man, Bad Soldier.[19] I still did not say anything. Then my brother went toward town and the man followed me home. We arrived at the place where my sister was living temporarily near Black River Falls.

After we arrived, the man took the water pail and went after some water. He got the water and brought it back and then later he went into the woods and brought back a lot of firewood. He began working for us, and sister was smiling broadly about it. He said to me, "If you would like it, tomorrow we can go to the courthouse and get our marriage license. If she hears about it, she will give up." He was talking about his wife. He had a wife and I did not want him, but he was persistent in courting me. "We will go to the courthouse and take out a marriage license so that woman cannot bother us," he said. So, that is what we did, we went to the courthouse and took out a marriage license. It was early spring when we did this.[20]

CHAPTER V

🌿 CONVERSION TO PEYOTE

At the time they built the dam at Hatfield, Wisconsin, we went there to live. My husband worked there, taking care of the horses. They used many horses. He used to wake up very early in the morning and be the first one on the job. He fed and harnessed the horses and prepared for whatever the workmen were going to do. Then he would come home to eat and go back again. We were there all summer long and he worked steadily. Then in the fall there was a fair and some of the people said that they were going to go dancing. My husband said, "Suppose we go too?" "All right," I said. So we went dancing with a white man they called Tom Roddy. We went to two or three different towns and then we finally reached Milwaukee where we used to dance. The gathering place where we danced was called Wonderland Park. Now when I ask about it, no one knows about it. That must have been a long time ago.

Eventually we became bored. My husband said, "Shall we go back?" We got together our bedding, blankets, suitcase and clothing and he said, "Now we will go back." Then we stole away. Green Horn was with us. He carried one of our suitcases. There was a high wire-mesh fence and we threw our suitcases on the other side. We threw over the things my husband carried on his back. He rolled up the blankets and we threw that bundle over too. The men climbed up over the fence.

My husband said, "Is it going to be all right for you?" "Yes," I said, "it is going to be all right. I am going to come across." —The men began walking on and I tucked my skirt between my legs like trousers and I climbed up the fence and over the top. When we were over on the other side we came upon some train tracks and following the tracks we headed for some woods. We walked along the tracks and reached the town. There we rode in a bus until we came to the depot and then we took the train to Black River Falls.

We did this in the fall and it was in the fall that they gave out money.[1] At that time I said, "I am going to go to Nebraska." I got a bundle and a trunk ready and asked my husband to take me to the depot. They took me there and then I just went off to Nebraska. I arrived at the place where my sister lived. They call it Wakefield, Nebraska. My husband had said, "If it is possible at any time I will come there." He did so later in the fall.[2]

There it was that we ate peyote. My husband never thought much of the Indian customs and whatever there was he mocked. But there he ate peyote and he realized something. Whatever the peyote was, he understood, and from that time we ate peyote.[3] I had two children at that time and I was going to have my third child. When I had children I used to suffer. I used to have a hard time and really suffered until I finally gave birth. There in Nebraska in the wintertime when we were with my sister I was about to give birth. I told her, "I think I am going to be sick." She said, "Little sister, when people are in that condition they use peyote. They have children without much suffering. Perhaps you can do that. You always suffer so much. This way you will have it easily."

"All right, whatever you say, I will do." That was the first time I was to eat peyote. My sister did that for me. She prepared it for me and gave me some and I took it. Then I soon had the baby. I had a boy.[4]

From that time on whenever they held peyote meetings we all attended. Mother, father, we all used to attend the peyote meetings. One time something happened to me. I had three children then and I used to be rather shy.[5] In the evening if I sat in the meeting, that would be all I did. I would just sit there. I would sit there all night. In the morning when they went outside, then I would go out too. It used to be hard for me. Some got up any time and went outside. But I used to think if I stood up, everybody would look at me. I used to respect people. Once when I was eating peyote,—I ate quite a bit, perhaps twenty buttons,—this is what happened to me.

I was sitting with bowed head. We were all sitting with bowed heads. We were supposed to ponder. We prayed. We were all doing this. We were having our peyote meeting. In the west the sun thundered and made terrible noises. I was hearing this sound. Oh, the sky was very black! I had my head bowed, but this is what I saw. The sky was terribly black. The storm clouds came whirling. When the storm clouds came the sky would become black. Big winds came. —The ground kept caving in. This is the way I saw it. It thundered repeatedly and the sky was dark. The storm was approaching and people came running. The women had shawls about them and they had bundles on their backs. They were carrying something on their backs, and they came running. There was a mighty wind and their clothes were blowing about them. They stumbled and rolled over and over. Then they would get up and run again. And there they came by. It did not seem to me as if it were windy. That is what I was seeing. And I thought to myself, ''Where are they fleeing? Nowhere on this earth is there any place to run to. There is not any place for life. Where are they saying that they are fleeing to? Jesus is the only place to flee to.'' That is what I thought.

Then I saw Jesus standing there. I saw that He had one hand raised high. The right hand, high in the air. I saw that He was standing there. Whatever He was doing, I was to do also. I was to pray, I thought. I stood up. Though I was in the midst of all those people my thoughts were not on that. I stood up because I saw Jesus. I will pray to Him, I thought. I stood up and raised my arm. I prayed. I asked for a good life,—thanking God who gave me life. This I did. And as the drum was beating, my body shook in time to the beat. I was unaware of it. I was just very contented. I never knew such pleasure as this. There was a sensation of great joyousness. Now I was an angel. That is how I saw myself. Because I had wings I was supposed to fly but I could not quite get my feet off of the ground.—I wanted to fly right away, but I could not because my time is not yet completed.

Then the drummers stopped singing. When they reached the end of the song they stopped. Then I sat down on the ground. I knew when I ate peyote that they were using something holy. That way is directed toward God. Nothing else on earth is holy. If someone speaks about something holy he does not know what he is talking about. But if someone sees something holy at a peyote meeting, that is really true. They are able to understand things concerning God. I understood that this religion is holy. It is directed toward God. I even saw Jesus!

After we had been in Nebraska about a year we lived at the home of my older sister Hiṅakega and her husband. My husband used to go out husking corn. Then in the spring we went to visit my aunt. Dog Howling she was called. My aunt was also my husband's niece. Her husband's name was Sound Of Thunder. He said to my husband, ''There is something you can do. You are a good worker, you can farm. You can go to the agency and rent some land to farm.—Then I can let you have one of my horses and you can pay me whenever you have the money.'' That is what he did. He went to the agency there in Nebraska.

Among my relatives there was a man named Little Wolf. He had some land out in the country. The family lived near the town of Winnebago but Little Wolf's land was out toward the town of Emerson. He had eighty acres with a house and a barn. That is what he rented to us. We lived there and they let us charge the cost of horses. We had a lot of little things and the people gave us furniture. There we lived and there my husband farmed. We were going to make a living for ourselves. I planted a vegetable garden. Then we had our oldest boy and he died. Then Hénaga, our second boy was born and he died while he was still small. Then Hínuga, the first daughter was born and then Hágaga, the third son. There we farmed and whenever there was a peyote meeting we attended it.

On one occasion my husband gave me four dozen chickens. He said, ''This is from the last of my mother's money that was at the agency. I did this because I thought that you would like it. If my mother were living she would not begrudge you anything she had. That is why I did this. I bought four dozen chickens with this money.'' He brought chickens for me and so I used to care for a flock of chickens. When they laid eggs I gathered them and in the spring I tended to the nests. We were getting along there quite well. In the fall he would have the huskers come including white men, and he would have them husk corn. There was a lot of corn. There it lay reaped, high like a hill, and after he had it husked they loaded it in a big wagon. He covered it and hauled the wagon to Thurston to sell the corn. He did this several days in a row.

Once I said, "How much are you earning from what we are doing?" He replied, "I paid for what we owed during the year. We owed several hundred dollars." We were paying our bills with all that corn he had been hauling. We had charged mules and even a big wagon and all kinds of big equipment. We must have owed many hundreds of dollars. That is what he was paying.

"Oh," I said, "I have been thinking and have reached this conclusion. Here we get up early in the morning and we farm and we continue doing this until nighttime. Even in the evening we work in this way. But we never see any money. That is what I think. Never any money! If we lived in Wisconsin and picked things as they do there we would have our money. Here we say we are farming and we make money for the white people and we never see any money.[6] I do not like this," I said.

"Well," he said, "we are our own masters. Who is boss over us?" Then he said, "I thought of something we might do." "All right," I said. So, we sold the machinery and bought an automobile. He bought a car there in Nebraska and we went west to where the Sioux lived, near a town called Merriman, South Dakota. There we went to live and we rented a house and we lived there. People trapped there. Once a man named White Thunder and his wife came to us and they lived there too. They used to trap. There were a number of lakes where they used to trap muskrats. Another man named Last To Come came to us and used to trap too. They did fairly well. Muskrat hides were seventy-five cents and soon, in two or three days, they could trap a hundred. So they did quite well.

After we had been there for a while the Sioux adopted me.[7] This was at Martin, South Dakota, where the Sioux lived. Peyotists used to come to us. We used to eat peyote with them. They even used to bring their sick people and we used to have peyote meetings for them. We rented a big house with White Thunder because the peyotists were coming to us. Later my husband rented a house in town and we lived there. He worked for a white man who had a big general store, a grocery store and butcher shop. My husband worked for him. He took a truck and went to the Indians. The Sioux reservation was quite a distance and he used to go there with groceries to buy cowhides from the Sioux. He used to trade food for hides. It was difficult for the Sioux to get to town. When they came to town with their wagons to buy food they had to sleep there overnight. Therefore my husband would visit the Sioux, trading food for cowhides. The man who employed him bought the cowhides. We must have lived there about two years and he had a good job.

Once he said, "When spring comes they are going to have an election for the position of mailman. They put my name with the rest. Whoever gets the most votes will be the mailman." Some time later he said, "I was elected to the position of mailman. I am going to start with a salary of eighty dollars a month."

However, I was lonely. I had thought we would return home and I said, "Stay here and be the mailman!" Then I began crying. "As for myself, I am going to go home. I have a lot of relatives. I am lonesome for my relatives, my brothers and my sisters. I am not going to stay here. Stay here and be the mailman!"

"Oh," he said, "I thought that you would be pleased. You have a lot of relatives here." When they adopted me they gave me four horses, some very fine horses. They thought a lot of me, those Sioux brothers, sisters and uncles. But I was lonesome. I wept when I said I was going to go back.[8]

"Well then," he said, "it can be that way. Who is our boss? We can do that. We can go back." He then sold all the household goods at the place where we were living.

White Thunder had become annoyed with us for some reason and that had made me unhappy too. My husband said, "We are going to go home. I am sending some of the things on the train this evening. I am sending the trunks back on the train. We ourselves will take only the good things like the blankets. I am going to send the things and we will go home without telling them. They do not like us."

"All right," I said.—We left early the next morning without telling anybody. Whatever the circumstances, I am always the one who is spoiling things.[9] If we had stayed there I would have learned to speak Sioux. We probably both would have learned to speak Sioux. Instead I thought more of my relatives and so we came back to Nebraska.

We came back to my sister's place and lived there. Then my husband said, "Let us go back to Wisconsin." My older brother, Hágaga, then said, "We want to go back to Wisconsin too, but wait until I do a few things and then it will be time to go." There they made my older brother a peyote leader. They gave him the peyote paraphernalia. Then we came back.

We came back to Black River Falls. In Wisconsin they hated the peyote people. We came back and some people did not even talk to us. The only people who would talk to us were our closest relatives. People supposedly said that we were not to live any place and not live together. They were going to scatter us. They watched us with harmful intent.

Tom Roddy in town used to like the Indians.[10] The Indians were his friends. He had land below the mission. They called

it "Frog Place." [11] "Live there," he said, "nobody is going
to say anything to you." So we went there to live. Then Little Thunder, Crosses The Sea and other people who preached
to each other came there from Nebraska. Wherever there were
peyote people they all came forth. There were quite a few of
us. We used to have meetings. Every Saturday night we had a
meeting. Every time we had a meeting someone got up and
testified. A woman named Walks Through The Village testified
and told about what we were going to experience. It was good
to hear.

Every Saturday we used to have a peyote meeting. We had
a gunny sack full of peyote and that is why we were able to
have meetings every Saturday. My husband did not know
the songs very well nor did Young Thunder nor Thunders
Suddenly Amongst Us. Only older brother knew them but
they sang anyway and older brother was the leader. Black
Chief, Young Thunder's son, was a small boy at that time,
about four or five years old—so that must have been about
1908.

Eventually it was time to pick blueberries and we moved
away to pick blueberries. Then blueberry time was over. Wherever we lived, we peyote people lived together in a group.
After all, the others hated us. When the blueberry season
ended we moved back to live on land owned by Young
Thunder's wife, on top of a hill that used to be called White
Brow's land. We made ourselves some big tents. Then we
heard that the Nebraskans were coming. At the same time
the other people were getting ready to have a powwow. They
were saying, "If any of these peyote eaters come we will
beat them senseless." They were going to have a powwow
and we were going to have a peyote meeting.

At that time the Nebraskans had a lot of money from selling
their land and they were enjoying themselves. They filled two

train coaches with Indians. They even had their drums and they sang in the train, drumming loudly. They got off at Black River Falls. We went there with our wagons. Mother and father had a wagon and Young Thunder also had one. Thunders Suddenly Amongst Us had a wagon too. But how many could we bring? There were a lot of them. They used up all the wagons and then they filled a big hay rack. A big group of Nebraska Indians came. Eventually we were going to have a big peyote meeting. They came to us and brought a big teepee. Previously brother and others had cut big poles and trimmed them and covered them over with canvas,—so the visitors would have a tent to stay in.

Before we had the peyote meeting someone there foretold that at the beginning of the evening an old bull would visit us. "He is going to come to us," he said, "and then on the second night that we are going to meet, a black mule is going to come to us." They knew this.

Then it was time to put up the teepee. There were all kinds of Winnebago, Nebraskans and a lot of Wisconsin Indians. It was very pleasant. The medicine lodge people were at odds with us. We were there in such a pitiful state so that when our relatives came we were very happy. We were cooking all about trying to feed everybody. Industrious women were there too and did a lot of cooking. They even brought their own food.

Then it was evening and time for the bull to come. In the evening before they went inside the teepee, a horse-drawn wagon used for hauling wood arrived, kararaš! It was a drunken man—and he just came running with the horses. He was singing and he turned in there. "Get in your children! The children!" they all shouted. The tents were scattered quite a distance around the teepee and he drove around the teepee. He was an old man driving a white horse. The old man had very white hair. He came running the horse. They spoke with him gently for a while and eventually they let him go home unharmed.

Then we held the peyote meeting and the teepee was full. Those that hated us came and saw their relatives who had come from Nebraska. Those who were not peyotists and had talked about beating us came and visited in our midst. They came and visited us to see their relatives.[12]

We held our meeting for two nights and on the second night the black mule came, Ñaqiga the son of Light At A Distance. They used to call him Old Man Ñaqiga. He came there drunk. He jeered as soon as he arrived. My husband was a guide.[13] He said to the drunk, "Grandfather, sit down. Sit down. If you do not listen to me I am going to tie you up." The drunk became angry. He was violent. "Well," said my husband, "I told you grandfather. I told you in a very polite way, 'I am going to tie you up,' I said." There was a big tent attached to the teepee and he let him sit there at the entrance of the tent. He tied his arms in back of him and tied him to a tent pole. "All right, sit there. Whatever you are saying does not matter. You are going to frighten the children running around here. That is why I am saying this." There he sat and the meeting began.

Later on they asked someone to speak at the meeting. Squeaking Wing was going to be the one to speak. Then he stood up and gave thanks. "There is much to be thankful for," he was saying. "Our relatives here do not know God. These are my childhood friends. My nephews, these are my childhood friends. It is good."—He was thanking them that they brought peyote to Wisconsin. He said, "They are working for God. They are doing a good thing here. We came to them and this evening we are having a very fine meeting. God is doing this. This religion He started. If I spoke here all night

49

I could never say all that there is to say about God's word, there is so much good to tell."

Then the drunk said, "Yes! Yes, that is true! You are bad, very bad, a big drunk, a fighter, biting off people's noses! Yes, God made a lot of people! You are never going to bite off all the people's noses!" Squeaking Wing laughed, "That is my uncle who is speaking. What he is saying does not matter. He is just petting me." [14] And we continued through the night until day came upon us.

In the morning we again began cooking. Then from that place we were going to go back to Nebraska. Twice we stayed up until daylight. Peyotists continued to arrive. Some took peyote there for the first time. The local people, however, never said anything good about us.

We left Young Thunder and Thunders Suddenly Amongst Us there. We went to Nebraska when everybody left. Some of the Wisconsin Winnebago went to Nebraska with their relatives. We were in Nebraska for a while and then we returned. My husband and I returned and from that time we ate peyote. Brother also used to eat peyote,—but things have changed now.

At first, whoever had been living together had to stay together. The bad men reformed. The women also stopped being bad. They took their marriage vows seriously. They were like that but eventually two or three men left their wives. They did again as they had done long before. They even married other women.—Before that happened, however—, they all made a big building in Nebraska for their meeting place and there they used to hold their peyote meetings. They used to preach to one another there. They chose twelve men who were educated and there they used to read. They used to tell what God did when He came to earth. They used to preach in their group.

Later, one of the men who had left his wife built himself a new house. The men who had left their wives and married other women borrowed his old house. There they had their meetings.[15] There they established a peyote meeting place. All they did was sing. That was called the Half Moon rite. They began only with singing. They did not have any preaching along with it.

Over at John Rave's meeting place it was called the Cross Fire rite. That group preached among themselves. The fact that they were preaching to one another touched a sensitive spot and that is why some of them made their own peyote meeting place. Over there at the Half Moon place all they did was sing. That was the beginning of the Half Moon. Yes, the peyote religion was like that. Today the Half Moon is the only rite that is held. Eventually the old men dropped peyote. The young were the ones who continued it.

Only the Half Moon continues today and the peyote leader himself was driven out. They drove him out, they scolded him. That is what they did. "What is he doing for us?" they said. That was my brother, Big Winnebago,—the one the white people call Crashing Thunder. However, he said, "There is only one God. I am old. I cannot sit up all night long. It is all right. I do not mind." Today he belongs to the church; "In the church I listen to a little preaching." That is what he does today, my older brother.—Today the young boys have that Half Moon peyote meeting—, and it is a good religion. They are getting along quite well and they have all made homes for themselves.[16]

As for myself, I am a member of the church at Black River Falls. My children went to school there when they were small and there they became Christians. There they were baptized and there we usually live.

CHAPTER VI

ꙮ WE LIVE AT BLACK RIVER FALLS

There was an empty house that my husband bought and dismantled. They brought back the lumber and my husband built a little shack.[1] We used to live there. He built a garage too. We lived on some land we intended to buy. They said it was forty acres and we said that we would buy it. That is why he built the house there. There was a white man and one time he said to my husband, "I bought this land. I am going to sell my land all in a parcel. I bought this land too." I got so mad.[2] I hated him. I really hated him. I said, "You have lived here a long time. Whatever land you were going to buy, it would seem that you would have bought it long ago. And now you have bought this land." I said this to that white man. So we took our house apart and moved across the way onto county land. There my husband rebuilt the house and we lived there. Later we lived on mission land.

At that time there was an old lady whom I knew. I wanted to visit her so we went to see her. This old lady was the sister of Get Up and her name was Hínuga, daughter of Laughs At Him. She lived with her grandson in a tarpaper wigwam across the road from the home of Get Up. The boy had lived with his parents in the tarpaper wigwam but they had moved some place else and only he and the old lady lived there. The tarpaper wigwam was full of holes and leaked when it rained. The floor was overgrown with grass. There was a little bed of some kind in the corner and she was sitting there. Her name was Hínuga Laughs At Him.[3] She was sitting there naked, wearing only a skirt. Her hair was all snarled and she never bathed. Nobody ever washed her and her body was streaked and dirty as if it were a map someone had drawn. I pitied her greatly. I sat next to her and put my arm around her. Her wrists were all crooked. Arthritis they call it. That is what she had.

"What is the matter with you?" I said. "You used to be a strong woman. What is the matter that you are in this condition?" I even fondled her hands. I pitied her so much. She wept, "No one ever did this for me before. They are afraid of me. Here I sit and you sit beside me and put your arm around me. You feel sorry for me. You are not afraid of me. You even touch me." That is what she said.

Oh, I really felt sorry for her. "Yes," I said, "I really pity you. I used to see you as a very strong woman and now you sit like this. I feel sorry for you. When I go to the agency I am going to tell them about you. I am going to tell them how I found you."—Then I cleaned her up a bit, combed her hair, put some clothes on her.

The agency was at Tomah and I wanted to go there so my husband took me there. We went there in our car. When we got there I told them there was an old lady who was to be pitied. They said, "Well, we'll look into the matter." I told them, "She is old, living in a leaky tarpaper wigwam." "We'll look at her," they said. The white people came there and built her a little shack and let her live in it. But she was in the same condition. They did not give her anything. The little boy cooked and that is all they ate. Again I told the agent, "She's in a shack but nobody looks after her. They don't even feed them." "Well," he said, "we're giving her eight dollars a month." "That is nothing!" I said. "But I am living near the mission and if it is possible to move her there, I'd take care of her." "Oh, won't that be nice!" the agent said. "Sure, you can ask whoever you think could move that house. Ask some people who have a team and I will pay them," he said.[4]

I asked three young men,[5] and they did it. They pulled the house. They hauled the house to the mission grounds near the spring. They pulled it to where we were living.

I took care of that old lady. I bathed her and took care of her in any way that I could. Once in a while I would give her medicine. Eventually she became stronger. She moved her fingers. She could fix her hair. She always said, "Oh, you certainly did something wonderful for me. I will never be able to do anything as good for you. Why, I might even have been dead by now!"

—One whole winter I took care of her. Then toward summer she said—, "Well, now I can help myself. I am able to care for myself because I am able to use my hands. I have a house at Dells Dam. My home is there. Move me to my house. I always hoped to go back there. I used to live there. Then I will see my little house." So that is what we did for her. We moved her to that place. I cleaned up her house and we came back, leaving her behind. A neighbor and his son stayed with her. The neighbor said, "I will stay here and look after them," and he lived there with them. He had a small boy too.

In the fall that little boy went to school at Neillsville,[6] so she was all alone. But in the fall they talked about going hunting. My husband said, "Let us go hunting." We went up north, trapping and deer hunting. Therefore, I asked here and there where they could take care of her for a while. At one house they said they would take that old lady temporarily. I would take her again when I came back. They kept her there. They called for her and took her back to their home.

We went up north and it was beginning to get cold, almost winter, when we came back.

They were afraid of her at that house, just as she had said earlier that people feared her. They were afraid of catching her sickness. They put her bed off to the side by the door. They left the door open and caused her to get a chill. She was dead when we returned, and my heart ached when I heard it. They were saying, "She died. Hínuga died."

Then, one time, my older son married a girl.[7] I told him not to do this, to marry some other woman. "There are girls who are good girls, you do not have to do this," I said. He did not listen to me and he got married but he did not remain married.[8]

At that time my husband was sick and was at the Tomah Hospital. Formerly there was a hospital there for the Indians and when they were sick that is where they went. Women who were going to have babies went there too. When my husband was sick that is where he went. His eyes were very sore and that is why he went to the hospital. Daughter-in-law,[9] my older son's wife also came to the hospital to have a baby. She had a little girl and this was my son's daughter. My husband was very happy because he had a granddaughter. When she cried he could recognize her crying. When she cried for a long time and it seemed as if she could not cry any longer he would become anxious about her over there,—where the babies were. He would go over there. When he went over there he would say, "Why is she crying?"

Daughter-in-law would say, "Oh, I am tending to her, that is why she is crying. I bathed her and put some fresh clothes on her."

"All right," he would say, and then he would go back.

Eventually she took the baby home to where she lived at her mother's place. She took her back there. After while, about two months later, I once saw a distant uncle of mine at Black River Falls. He was called Charley Lowe Cloud [10] and he was married to my daughter-in-law's mother. He said, "My niece, let me tell you something."

"All right," I said.

"Niece," he said, "I am going to tell you some bad news. Your daughter-in-law goes out early in the evening. She goes away and is gone all night. Your grandchild cries there upstairs all night. I do not like to hear that. Since I am related to you in this way, I thought that if you heard about it, perhaps you might claim your grandchild. That is why I told you this. I thought that if you had your own grandchild you would take good care of it. So, I told you. I thought that I would help you to this extent, niece. That is why I told you this." That is what he said.

I went over there immediately and when I arrived daughter-in-law was there. Before the baby was born I had bought little blankets for her. I bought clothes and diapers for the baby. Whatever clothes were necessary, I had bought for the baby. I said, "I came for my granddaughter." I guess she must have known why I came there. She must have known that I heard what she was doing. She did not say a word. She just bowed her head. I gathered together all of the child's belongings. I put clean diapers and clothes on the baby. I put the baby's clothes in a suitcase. I wrapped her up and took her home.[11] Daughter-in-law did not even say a word. I took the baby when she was two months old and reared her to adulthood. She went to school and when she finished eighth grade she went away to high school at Flandreau, South Dakota.[12]

Then we once moved from the county land to near the mission and built a house there. At the time we moved my husband repaired his car. It was very cold but he fixed the rings and lay on the ground under the car. There he caught cold and coughed and coughed. At that time my older brother [13] was working in Washington, D.C., and he came back for a visit. He said, "You could go back with us if you wish. My brother-in-law's health is not good, and he might possibly get better there." So, we went back with him. But he became progressively worse so we returned to live at our home.

He was sick almost all winter. My older sister, Bald Eagle, was also sick. They said there was no hope for her. She was sick and one time my husband said, "Oh, poor Xórajawiŋga is standing outside the door. She is to be pitied. She wants to leave with a man." He was teasing her.[14] Early the next morning somebody knocked and I opened the door and there was my nephew. "Auntie, mother died," he said. "Auntie, do not take it too hard. You are busy with uncle sick too."

"Yes, that is true," I said. My husband was on the other side of the house and I was on the side where the kitchen was located. I sat quietly in a chair.—I did not want to tell my husband about my sister because he was sick—, and later he said he had not heard my nephew. I was just sitting there and he said, "Little Siga?" "Yes," I said and came over there. He looked right at me and said, "Siga, I do not want to see you cry. I am not very strong. My will power is not very strong. I do not want to see you cry. If your heart aches for your sister, you have good reason. When they make wake donations, ease the pain in your heart at that time."

"All right," I said.

I did not tell him but he knew that my sister had died. Two days earlier he had foretold that this was going to happen. And after he died they built a house for me. He knew that too. He said, "Siga?" "Yes?" I said.

"Have they finished the house yet?"

"What house?"

"Oh, the house they are building for us."

"They are not making a house for us at any place. You must be dreaming about it."

"That may be. I thought they were building you a house," he said.

He knew that they were going to build me a house. It was not long after that and he said, "Little Siga, tomorrow I am going to be leaving all of you. It cannot be helped. That is the way it has to be."

My oldest daughter was there. Something must have been said about the illness because early in the morning an old lady named Eating Things came there. Then my husband said to me, "Sit over here." I sat on the edge of the bed. "I tried to pray," he said, "but I cannot. Pray for me."

"All right," I said. I prayed, saying we could not help ourselves in our present condition. I gave us all over to God's will. That is how I prayed. I left the sick man in Jesus' hands. I could not help myself. It must be as God decided. That is what I said.

He was thankful. "You spoke well," he said, "that is what I wanted to say. You spoke well." After a while I stopped praying.

His eyes did not look good. His eyes were clouded over. There was a rattling noise in his throat, "xíti, xíti, xíti." And in his chest something went, "xic, xic, xic." "What is it that is making that noise?" he said. He was making all those sounds because his breathing was stopping. Then his breathing stopped, it was smothered out.

—Then I told my girl who was in the other room, "My dear daughter, your daddy has passed away." My daughter came in. "Daddy," she cried. "Daddy!" and she cried and cried.

The old lady was still with us. "It cannot be helped," she said. "It cannot be helped.—You know, your mother was praying and gave everything to God. Everything is God's will. We are Christians. We accept everything God is doing. Do not cry.'' And my daughter stopped crying.

It was April 24, 1936, that my husband died. We told the undertaker,[15] who took him and brought him back. They buried him in the mission cemetery. In the evenings I used to think as I sat there, ''Maybe this is not happening to me. Maybe this is not happening to me. Maybe he did not die.'' Children of mine died. My relatives died, father and mother. My older sister died. But it was never as hard as when my man died. ''Maybe I am having a bad dream,'' I thought. I would pinch my arms to see if I were awake.

Then the doctor came. He used to come and see my husband when he was sick. He came there and said to me, ''Have them dismantle this house and build it someplace else. Your husband had double pneumonia and tuberculosis set in. That is what he died of. Tear down your house and build it over. You have a lot of small children. Don't stay in this house.''

So, one time I was sitting on the roof of the house with a hammer. The roof was covered with tarpaper and I was trying to get it off. A car came by and then it turned back. It was one of my nephews and another young man. ''What are you doing, auntie?'' he said.

''This house has to be taken apart to move some place else. I am supposed to get it rebuilt. I am trying to get the roof off.''

''Oh, auntie, we will do that for you,'' he said, and they got out of the car and started to work. They took the whole house apart. They stacked the boards. They went home in the evening and they came back early in the morning. They took everything apart and piled the boards on top of each other. They said, ''Aunt, where are you going to have them build the house?''

''Well, let it be on the mission grounds,'' I said. Then they told me that it was partly government land. "Put it there," I said, and pointed out the spot to them and they hauled the boards over there. They certainly did me a great kindness.

Then I went to town to the lumber company and I said to the owner, "I get a little money once a year. How would it be if I would charge some doors and some windows?"

He said, "You aren't supposed to help yourself. Go to Harry Perry, he'll tell you." [16] He must have telephoned him. I went there to Harry Perry. He is dead now. I told him, "I am supposed to take the house apart and build it some other place."

"Oh, they'll do that for you," he said. "Don't try to help yourself. They'll do that for you." Then he sent word to the agency. He made a telephone call to the agency. The next morning the agent and another man came. "How big a house do you want?" they said.

Across from the airport [17] there was a little square house. I told them that I always liked that house. It was not too big and it was not too small. "I have a lot of little children and when my married children come back with their families I am crowded. Two of them with their children come home to visit. I used to be crowded. That square house is just about the right size. I like that one." They went to look at it. They said I was right, that house was the right size. They made my little square house. There was no one around who could build houses, so the Indian boys got together and made the house. They finished it for me and I am living there today. That is how I got the house where I live.

After I managed it, they made houses for others who did not even help themselves with one nail. They made houses for them. But the agent from Ashland said my case is the same as theirs. I do not know why, but whatever the white people say, that is the way it has to be. I guess it must be that way.

CHAPTER VII

MEDICINES AND A VISION[1]

There was an old man who was my grandfather,[2] and I used to help him in various ways. I always gave him food. He liked to eat. That is the way old people are. If you give food to an old person and he really likes it, that is very good. The thinking powers of old people are strong and if one of them thinks good things for you, whatever he wishes for you, you will obtain that good fortune. That is what they always said. I used to give things to this old man. He wore buckskin moccasins, he always wore Indian shoes. He did not like hard-soled shoes, so I used to make buckskin moccasins for him. He appreciated whatever I did for him. If I ever went to a town and there was a secondhand store I always looked at the pants, big pants, and if a pair seemed the right size, and a shirt, I bought them. I would give them to him. "Grandfather," I used to say to him, "I brought these things for you."

"Oh, granddaughter," he used to say, "you are doing a great kindness."

Quite often I did things of that sort for him. I often fed him. If he were coming by on the road when it was close to mealtime I would call to him, "Grandfather, come and eat."

"Oh, good!" he would say. He would come and eat there and he would be so grateful.

Sometimes if there was a coat that seemed the right size, one of those nice overcoats, if I could afford things of that sort

I would buy them and give him such things. One time there were some white people who had a little cookstove. It was small, about eighteen inches square,[3] and made of cast iron. I thought that little range was very cute. I asked the white people, an elderly married couple, "Would you be interested in selling your stove?"

"Well," they said, "once in a while we cook outside when the house is hot and we use it when we are outside." They discussed it. "What do you think?" they asked each other. Then the old man said to his wife, "Well, it's yours. What do you think?"

"Oh?" she said, "I'm glad you told me that!" Then that white woman said to me, "How much would you give me for it since you're asking me about it?"

"I'll give you four dollars," I said to her.—I just said that, I did not think she would take it—,[4] and she said, "Ok."

I gave her four dollars for that little stove. I thought it was cheap. We put it in the trunk of the car and went home. It was a good stove. It even baked very good biscuits. Then we took that stove to the old man: "Grandfather, we brought you a stove. It would be nice if you could cook some food for yourself. It would be nice if you could boil some things and bake some bread for yourself. Although the people next door to you usually feed you, they are always talking about it. Now you can cook for yourself."[5] We put the little stove in his tarpaper wigwam.

"Oh, granddaughter," he said, "I am glad you have told me of this. Now I will be able to cook for myself," and that is what he did. Then he said, "Granddaughter, you have helped me with many things. What do you wish? You have helped me in many ways and given me many things. What is it that you want? Tell me. Merely the fact that you give me food is good. You give me food and ask me to eat and you even give me clothing. You have certainly treated me very well. You have done many kindnesses for me. Tell me whatever it is that you want.''[6]

"Yes, grandfather, I always liked the Indian medicines. I have a lot of children and I even have grandchildren. I do not always have money to pay for the doctor. I know it is a fact that the Indian medicines help people. I always liked the Indian medicines.''

"Oh, granddaughter, you have certainly said something worthwhile. You have asked for a very good thing. You said a good thing. You are going to have something valuable. I am old, I feel sorry for my medicines. I am thinking, it is going to be the end of these medicines. That is what I am thinking and my heart is sad for them. My son does not care for Indian medicines. He does not think much of Indian medicines. He uses only one medicine, peyote.[7] He thinks that it cures whatever is wrong with him. He cares nothing for those Indian medicines. What you are saying is very good, granddaughter. I like that. A long time ago when you were a little girl this was meant to occur. Way back then you were working for it. When mother used to give medicines to the white people you used to help her by being her interpreter. Since that time these medicines were going to be yours. You have been working for them since long ago. You have been working for this. Today it has come about.

"It is good. You will prescribe Indian medicines. I used to do this; now you will do it. The power will all be yours. You are not yet holy, but these medicines are holy.''—I did not know what he meant by that, but he said—, ''These medicines are going to talk to you. If someone sets his mind on you, that is, he is going to buy medicines from you, you will know it before they come to you. And when they come to you, say to them, 'You will be cured.' If you put your mind to it intensely, that is where you will have your power. Then you will give them Indian medicines. You are going to be a medicine woman. You are going to cure sickness. This redounds to your honor, my granddaughter.''

This is what my grandfather said to me. Ńaqisáneiŋgahínigra, Náqiwaŋkwaxópiniga, he was called.[8] I learned his medicines. He told me all of them, so I know a lot of good medicines.[9]

At one time I thought it was just empty talk when they spoke about old religious ways.[10] Once they said they were going to have a scalp dance, a victory dance. They were going to have a feast and dance with the scalp. One of the scalps was going to come back, they were saying.[11] Later they brought me the patchwork covering of a quilt. It was an invitation that they brought me. I was to dance with the quilt top. I was very pleased. I was not very important yet they brought this to me.[12] I was very happy when I realized that they were coming to me and that they brought this for me. They always say that when they do this they do it in honor of their male relatives. I thought to myself, I believe I am expected to help in this matter. I went to town and bought some meat, a kettleful of beef, and I also bought bread. My children took me to the place in the evening and I gave the things to my uncle. ''I brought this to fill a kettle,'' I said.

''Oh, niece, you did a great kindness, thank you very much,'' he said.[13]

''And here is a dollar,'' I said, ''use it for this thing which you are doing.''

''Oh, niece, thank you very much.'' It was Last To Emerge [14] who said this, and it was his scalp dance.

In the evening they had a victory dance. They dance outside. I was right in the midst of things with my quilt top. I danced and when they were finished with the victory dance and the sun was going down they then danced around the lodge and everybody danced. We danced all around the lodge and then we went inside the lodge. They put the drum down and they stuck in the ground the stick to which the ornamented scalp was attached. In the course of the ceremony people are invited to dance with the scalp, and I danced with the scalp.

It came time for the feasting and they ate. Then the night dancing was begun. All night long we danced. Outside there were a lot of automobiles. This is something I think and this is why I am telling it. Long ago whenever they did this they did everything in the proper way. But now, late at night, everybody left one by one. It would seem that people would do things as they are supposed to do them, but they went away. The only ones remaining were Cloud Over There, Queen Of Thunder, and Water Spirit Woman. Those people who were leaving were going to bed in their tents outside and they were even sleeping in the cars. When day began to break we sang as loudly as we could so that with our singing we would awaken those who were sleeping. We were singers. Three women singers were left and Cloud Over There, the man who was supposed to give the war whoop at the end of the songs. He would do this. We were doing things according to the rules. It seemed we peyotists were the only ones who were left and who were dancing. They saw us, but that is the way they behaved, those people who were holding the dance. They did not obey the rules.

In the morning, at dawn, they stop dancing until noon when they have a victory dance. So, I went home. My family came for me and I went home. Before noon I told them to take me over there again. When it was noon they had a victory dance. There is a pole outside and they hang the drums on this pole and sing the victory songs. There we danced again.

We were dancing with the scalp. Then I went home for only a little while to do whatever work I had to do at home. It was the afternoon and that is why I went back. I think I probably slept for a little while too. I lay down for a while as I was tired.

Again in the evening I said, "All right, take me back over there again." My children took me over there. Once more they had the victory dance outside and eventually they stopped singing and at nightfall they prepared the things to eat. Again they put on the kettles. Then they began dancing once more. They began dancing and finally they sang the victory songs. We danced all night and the same thing happened. Again they disregarded the rules. That is, the ones who invited us, our paternal relatives. We were behaving according to tradition. We thought we were supposed to dance. We were peyote people but we stayed up until daylight. The other women left. That is what they did. They went to sleep. They held nothing sacred. They just behaved in that casual way. The men were the same way.

It was a pitiful thing to see the one in charge of the ceremony. He was offering tobacco. He was crying as he sat there, —humbling himself before the spirits, asking for life. Those who were sitting across from him teased among themselves, teasing and laughing loudly. Oh, I heard them! I used to think they considered nothing sacred. They knew nothing of respect. That is what I thought of them, those conservative people.[15]

I used to attend conservative ceremonies regularly. One Horn used to invite me to eat from his kettle. I went to feasts when my brother-in-law invited me. I used to be given meat and I used to eat. When he died I did not go to feasts any more. They did not have any respect at that time either. They were just doing that,—without feeling any reverence for it. They still hold feasts that way to this day.

They held the scalp dance for two nights and on the second night when day overtook us, I came home. When they brought me back to my home I was not even sleepy. But we had a little narrow cot in the kitchen and I went there to lie down. My granddaughters said, "Grandmother, are you tired?" I was not really sleepy and I said, "I am just resting for a little while. I am not very tired but I am going to lie down here."

"All right, grandmother, I am going to close the door," one of them said. She closed the door, they said, so they would not disturb me. I lay there, closing my eyes now and then. I became rather drowsy but I did not sleep deeply. Suddenly, there was a young man with blond hair combed back in a wavy pompadour. He was a handsome young man and he was wearing a soldier's uniform. He had on a khaki jacket and he had his hands in the pockets. Oh, he was dancing, dancing the way everyone else was dancing! He began dancing and I saw him glance at me. "Oh, we beat you!" I said. "We beat you. That is why we are dancing at your expense,—with your scalp. Whatever power you had is all going to be ours because we beat you!" I sat up. I was startled. That is what I saw.

Later, when we ate, we invited my nephew Lone Man to eat with us. I told him what I had seen. "Well, aunt," he said, "you respected that scalp dance from the beginning. You were still taking part when it ended. You were there two nights. You spent the time properly. That is what you did. You spoke the truth when you said that we beat them, even in doing this you respected the scalp dance. Some do not respect it. They just remain for a short time. Some of them even go home during the dance. That is what they do. But, for as long as you were there, you were dancing. From the beginning you followed through to the end. Some of them do not even dance after a while. You were the only one left, and this did not go unobserved. You certainly spoke the truth. We won. That is why you were dancing with the scalp. Whatever good luck was to have befallen him we won for ourselves. You spoke well. You spoke the truth, aunt, when you said this." [16]

CHAPTER VIII

🌿 CHILDREN AND GRANDCHILDREN

My children are now all grown up. They were born here and there and I am going to tell about that too. I had eleven children. Three of them died, two boys and one girl. I now have thirty-eight grandchildren and nine great-grandchildren.[1]

Hínuga, Flies About, was born at Wittenberg, Wisconsin, and two years later Wíhanga, Flapping Wings, was born there.[2] I used to know how old they are but I do not even remember that any more. Then we went to Nebraska and there the oldest boy was born and also Hénaga, the second boy. They both died. Hínuga, White Hawk, was next. I had her when we lived where my sister, the wife of Gathering Of People, lived. Then we lived in another place where we fended for ourselves, and every time that I was going to have a baby I went back to my sister's place. We did not even have a doctor. I used to have my babies at my sister's home. There I had Hágaga, Lamb.[3] I came back to my sister's place. Wíhanga, Sweet Corn, I had at my sister's home and then we went to the Sioux.

There we lived by hunting. There my husband was given the job of which I spoke. Then I had Hakśigaga, Swift Water,[4] and then we came back to Wisconsin. When we returned we lived at Wisconsin Rapids and there I had Hinákega, Call Upon Her. She died. Then I had Náqiga, Came On Earth.[5] I had him at cherry land,—Door County—, at an orchard. He is named for the people who owned the orchard. When we lived there everybody went picking cherries. We lived in a tent.

Once some women were talking: ''Where is the tent that a little one was born? Do you have a dog?''

''No, come right in,'' I said. They came in when I called out to them. They were Oneida. I used to go to school with them when I went to school at Wittenberg. And there was an old white lady with white hair, the wife of the old man who owned the orchard. She had a big package. She said, ''They said that they gave my husband's name to the baby that they had here. I am very proud of that. A baby was never born here at the orchard. Here, I brought him some little clothes.'' Fluffy little white blankets, little sweaters, dresses, little white dresses and little shoes, little white stockings and diapers; that is what they brought him. He was named for the orchard owner. The wife, the old lady who said this, brought him clothes. There I had him.

Then I had Siǵax́unuga, Daylight, at Wisconsin Rapids.[6] At that time we lived just outside of town in a house that we rented. We were living there and I had my fifth daughter, my last child. I spoke of where I had my children and where they built me a house. There, at Black River Falls, my children went to school and I am living there today.

Today my children all live scattered over great distances. My oldest daughter lives at Wisconsin Rapids and my second daughter lives at Neillsville. Hínuga, White Hawk, lives at Waterloo, Iowa. My elder son married a woman from a different tribe called Shoshoni. He married a woman there and lived at Fort Washakie. His wife died but he is still living there with his children, his young girls. Sweet Corn used to live at Brigham, Utah. Then they said they were going to live at Sioux City, Iowa. Son-in-law was going to work for the state. And Swift Water lives at Stockton, California. Her daughter is married and has a child and lives in her own home. Her younger son lives with her and her older son is a soldier and is in Germany. This winter or maybe this spring he is going to be discharged and he said then he is going to visit me. I raised those children. My younger son lives between Lyndon Station and Wisconsin Dells, my youngest daughter lives in Milwaukee.[7]

At the time my granddaughter went to South Dakota to high school, during the war when they were enlisting men in the army, my son-in-law, the husband of one of my daughters, Swift Water, did not want to be a soldier.[8] He said, ''There is a lot of civilian work in connection with the war.''

''Yes, that is so,'' they told him. ''It is possible to work in Oregon. If that is what you are going to do, we can send you to Oregon.'' He said that is what he wanted to do. He did not want to be a soldier.[9] Instead he wanted to do war work. That is why they sent him and his wife and children to Oregon. My daughter had two older children, a boy and a girl, and a little baby boy. They went where they sent them to work at the edge of the ocean. He said he was going to work there.

He had a craving for liquor so I said when they were about to leave, ''Oh, you are going to be very far away. You are going to a distant place. You are going to the end of the world. You have a wife and children. Do not do there as you behave here. It is very far, that Oregon, I am not always going to know what you are doing. I am concerned about them. I am worried for my daughter—I can't reach over; too far for me.''

''Grandmother,'' [10] he said, ''it is so far where we are going that we will be concerned for each other. We are going

to be drawn to one another. Grandmother, do not worry."
Then I did not think it was going to be as it turned out. I
thought he meant what he said.

After a while my daughter was going to have a baby.—I
got a letter from my girl. She wanted me. "Mother, I would
like you to come. I will pay your fare," she said. We did as
she asked. We went there, my youngest daughter and my
granddaughter and I, before it was time for school to start.
We went there by train in two days and two nights. We were
taken over to where they lived. We rode in a taxi. I knew the
name of the place where they were and we arrived there. They
were very happy and the children were very happy. They saw
that I had come a great distance to get there. Oregon, that is
where I had gone.

Daughter said, "Mother, older brother is here."

"Oh, that is good," I said.

She said, "He is working. He is going to come back tomorrow."

In the morning he came back. "Oh, mother, you are here!
Mother, women work too where I am working. Can you work,
mother?" [11]

"Yes," I said, "I can work."

"They are being paid sixty-five cents an hour," he said.
"The women do not do a great deal, it is light work. They
cut grass and weeds there with a hoe and straighten out the
berry vines." That is what they were doing. He said it was
not hard. "Mother, you could go over there. There are a lot
of houses. My sister can work there too, and my wife can
come from where we are living. It is not far," he said. "If
you like, I will come for you tomorrow."

"Yes, we would like that," my daughter said.

In the morning he came for us with a truck. We were getting
all the things ready and we just packed everything in there.

After we had loaded up we went to the place where they picked berries. They were saying that everything was almost ripe, and we were going to pick all summer long. That is what we did. We moved over there. We lived in a two-story house that had a lot of rooms. That is what I did, I worked. There were white women there too and I just worked among them.[12] Every week we got paid on Friday. I must have worked about two weeks and then the raspberries were ripe. The vines were dotted with red berries. For a little while, perhaps a week, we did not work there. They said that the berries must be left alone. We were not to go among them. We did not work for about a week or perhaps a little longer. Then they said it was time to pick raspberries.

Then we used carriers that could hold six quarts. We carried those when we used to pick. When we filled the carrier we took it in and they punched a book that had numbers in it. They used to punch our books and I think a filled book was worth $2.50. We were doing this and then other kinds of berries became ripe,—boysenberries, great big berries. They look like a blackberry, but much bigger, kind of purple. They smell so good; taste so good—.

When we were finished with that a telegram came for me. This said that my son had been wounded, my son Náqiga who was in the army. They sent it. They said that he had been shot.

When he was ready to leave for the army he had said, "Mother, if something bad happens to me, if this ever happens to me, do not take it too hard. You believe in God. If they ever do anything to me, we will see each other wherever God is." My heart ached but I said to him, "Sonny, thank you. I will try." But now it was not anything to be thankful for. He said this to me when he was just about ready to leave. And then, there I was at the world's end picking berries. At that time they brought me the telegram that said my sonny was wounded. I did not know what to say. Then my youngest daughter became very pale and dropped to the floor. They picked her up and put cold water on her face. My daughters were crying, but I did not cry. I thought of what my son had been saying.

Then son-in-law said, "Grandmother, do not take it too hard. I do not want to see you feeling unhappy."

"All right," I said, "that is just what my son told me not to do when he was getting ready to leave."

"Well, that is good, grandmother. I am glad that I did not see you cry," son-in-law said.

Then I went picking when it was time to pick berries. It was early in the morning when they brought the telegram. I was the first one to go to the berry place. I thought to myself, I will go before the white people arrive. I went to where they had finished picking and when I got there I wept. I prayed to God and I cried as hard as I could cry. I was crying quite a distance from the other people. I cried as loud as I could and I cried as much as I wanted to. That is the way I cried. Then when I got enough crying, I stopped crying. When I stopped crying my anxiety seemed to be relieved. Then, after I cried it out, this pain in my heart, I felt better. I began picking and soon the white people began to arrive for the picking. After while many white people were there.

About noon my youngest daughter came there. You could see her coming along the crest of a hill. She was running, but ever so often she seemed to jump in the air. I thought to myself, why is she doing that? She is running sometimes almost playfully. What has she got to be happy about? As she came closer she yelled, "Mother! Mother! Brother sent a letter!" She was shouting this, running and skipping as she came along.

"Mother," the letter said, "they wounded me, but do not take it too hard. This way I will get back earlier to the States. Mother," he said, "then we will see each other soon. That is why I am writing this letter, hoping you will see it before you get the telegram. I wanted to let you know I was wounded before they sent the telegram to you. I hope that you will see this first. I wrote this as soon as I could." He said a telegram was sent too.

I was very happy, but my tears again fell.

We continued picking at that place and eventually he sent a letter. "Mother," he wrote, "I want you to come back to Wisconsin. I am back from overseas. I am back. I may be seeing you very soon. That is why I want you to come back to Wisconsin."

The berry season was almost over and then I was supposed to come back. My daughter said, "Mother, the trains are filled these days. Now that you are going back I will go to the depot to make a reservation for you on the train that you are going to take. That way you will have a seat."

"All right," I said.

"Mother, it is going to be very hard for me, but you must go home. My younger brother is right in saying this," she said.

I told her, "If you want us all to go back, we can just move on. Eventually, we will get back. We can buy a secondhand car. We can all go back. In time we will get home."

"No, mother," she said, "I certainly do not want that. When we were ready to leave home my husband was to have a very big job. That is how it was when we came. Today, how are we? We are unable to earn anything. I do not want the people to see me come back like this."

"All right," I said.

Two days later they took me to town,—to Portland. We

were going to go on an evening train. The train pulled into the station. There were many trains arriving and departing. My daughter took me to the one that we were going to board and we got on. When we got on I went in and sat down immediately. It was very hard for me to leave her that way, but I had to do it. Then she came toward me. There was an open window so I sat beside it. She cried as hard as she was able. She was standing between the trains and crying as hard as she could. I was as heartsick as I could be. But it could not be helped. My son had almost been killed so I was going home. I had to leave another child there. It was hard when we left. It was all I could do to leave. It was not until I was about halfway back that I could take my thoughts off of it.[13]

My little granddaughter said, "Grandmother, what is it that the people do when they call them to eat?" My daughter had filled a basket with all kinds of food for us. We had that with us. But my granddaughter said, "Grandmother, we never go there to the place where they go to eat."

"Oh, we have lots of food," I said, "but, all right, we can do as you wish." So that is what we did. We went to the fifth car; that was the dining car. There were little square tables. Two soldier boys were sitting there and we sat there too. There we sat, four of us. They were wearing khaki uniforms.

"Oh," I said, "I am going to eat with my sons. Whenever I see somebody wearing khaki, I always think that might be my son." I was speaking English.

The boy across from me got up. "My mother died when I was born. I never had a mother. Now I have a mother," he said. Then he shook my hand. He was very pleased that I said to him that he was my son. He was glad, he said, because now he had a mother.—I was glad too because I was feeling unhappy about my boy. "Well, boys, I am happy to know you,'' I said. ''I am glad too, mother,'' he said. Eventually we went back to where we were sitting.

After travelling a while we arrived at St. Paul where we changed trains. When we boarded a train there I was happy. I felt that I was home when we reached St. Paul. I was so happy to think that I was home. We had left from La Crosse, but when we returned we went directly to Black River Falls. There we got off the train and spent the night at a motel.

In the morning I went downtown and there I saw one of my daughters. ''Mother, did you come back?'' she said. ''Yes,'' I told her. ''Oh, mother, it is good that you came back! Mother, the old people [14] have come by already. They are going to have a medicine dance at Valley Junction, and that is where we are going. Just my daughter and I are going together. Let us all go there so you will see some people. You have been gone a long time.''

''All right,'' I said. I went along with them in their car. There I watched the medicine dance and I saw my sister. I stayed where she was camping. When it was over I went home.

—I stayed at home and my younger son came home once in the winter, about Christmastime. He was on crutches. He just came home for a little while and then he went back to the veterans' hospital. I was glad to see him. One side of his body was badly injured, his arm and two places on his leg. He had to stay in the hospital for a long time.[15]

Then, late the next winter I again received a letter. A woman wrote a letter to me. It said, ''I am taking care of your grandchildren and they are always talking about you. Your daughter left them because of her husband. He could not take care of them. They do not know where she went. They looked for her but they could not find her. The man cannot take care of the children so I am taking care of them. I am taking care of your grandchildren. They are always talking about you and I asked them, 'Would you like to see your grandmother and she will take care of you?' They said, 'Yes.' I said, 'All right, I will write her a letter.' ''

She wrote me a letter and when the letter came my heart ached. Tears came to my eyes and I cried very hard. That is the way I am. I was feeling so sad about my daughter that she went through this misfortune. I was very sad.

I went to town immediately. There was a woman in town who thought a great deal of me.[16] When I got there I let her see the letter. ''Do you want to go after them?'' she asked me.

''Yes,'' I said.

''Well, you can do that. You can go after them. When will you be ready, right away or tomorrow?''

''I will go home and get ready, and then I will go tomorrow.''

''You do that,'' she said. ''Tomorrow everything will be ready for you, your fare too,'' she said.

I was very glad. I went home and bathed and packed two sets of clothes in a suitcase. I went back in the morning and they took me to the train immediately. I left on the ''400,'' a fast train they call it. I got on that train and then I changed trains at St. Paul where I got on another fast train. I used to think it was fast when I used to see it go by so quickly. They called it a fast train but now I did not think it was fast because I was very anxious to reach my grandchildren. I arrived at daybreak after two nights. On the second day at daybreak, about three o'clock I got to the town of Yakima, Washington. That is where I arrived.

The woman who had sent me had written a telegram to a woman there. She had said to me, ''They will meet you.'' I arrived at daybreak and at the town I saw a sign for a hotel. There was a hotel close to the depot that I headed for. I went there to sleep. I slept until about eight or nine o'clock. I got up and went downstairs. When I asked for the dining room they said to me the place was just for sleeping, but that there was an eating place close by. I left my bag there and started off for the place they told me about and I went to eat.

After I finished eating I asked them where the welfare office was located. They said, "If you take this street you will get to the main street. There you go east and then you will be able to see it across the street. You can see where it says, 'Welfare Office.' "

"All right," I said, and I asked when it was open. They said people start going in about ten o'clock.

So, that is what I did. I went back to the hotel and asked for my bag. After while when it was almost ten o'clock I started out. As I walked through town I looked about as I went along. I looked in the store windows and continued on in this fashion. Finally I saw what they had told me about. I saw it in the distance and there was also a clock there. The clock said about a quarter after ten. I went over there and when I got there I went in. People were already there and they were standing in line at a window. Some were sitting on benches and some were sitting on chairs. Then one of them who was sitting next to me said, "You must be a stranger here."

"Yes," I said, "I came from Wisconsin." [17]

People were standing in a long line and still more people were coming in. At last I got to the window. I gave the name of the woman whom they had told me to ask for. I asked if she were there. The girl said, "She hasn't come in yet. When she comes I will tell you. Sit down there. She is expecting you." She even knew my name. "She will be glad to see you." So, I sat down.

People kept going by, walking up to the window for papers. Finally they called my name. I went over there and they opened a door for me to go in. I went in and the woman was standing there. "I did not think you were going to get here this soon," she said. She named a different hotel and said, "I expected you there instead. That is why I did not meet you. It is too bad."

"It doesn't make any difference," I said, "I saw this hotel and I slept there."

"Well, it would have been nice if I could have been there," she said. She was very sorry. Then she said, "After dinner we will go to where the children are staying. But first we will go together to the Indian agency." She had a car and we got into it and went to the Indian agency. We sat down there. She was talking to the agent, telling him about me. She was even talking about my son-in-law. Ever so often Indians came in, young people. They had very nice clothes. The young girls even had leather jackets. They were nicely dressed. They were Indians but they were not good looking, not even the young boys.

We came back after a while and she visited around town. She even looked at things in the stores. "Didn't you bring any kind of blanket?" she said to me.

"No," I said.

"Look around, you might buy a blanket. When you take the children back on the train you can cover them when they sleep," she said.

"Yes, I can do that," I said. She gave me some money, sixty-five dollars she gave me.

"Use this, you probably won't be getting any help right away when you get back. You are taking the children and I'd like to give you more but this is all I have." She gave me sixty-five dollars. I said I had my return fare. "But the oldest child, I don't know whether you will have to pay for him or not," she said.

"No, they are all small," I said to her.

Then we went to get the children at the place where they were staying. I knew the name of the woman but I have forgotten it. We went about fifteen miles. There was a farm house; that is where they were. We called for them there. The woman was in the habit of caring for children. Wherever it was, there were a lot of fruit trees. There was no other kind of land, only orchards. When we arrived the children were very happy.

"Oh, grandma, I didn't think I was going to see you so soon! Grandma, we are so happy to see you!" [18] The older ones, Kúnuga and Hínuga, their eyes filled with tears. I kissed them and Hénaga and Wíhaŋga too. Wíhaŋga was only two years old. She was just sitting there. Then I said, "I came for you. We will be going home."

"Oh, grandma, is that so?" They were very happy. Hínuga skipped about she was so happy. "Oh, grandma, really?"

The woman said, "I liked taking care of them very much. They are never disobedient. I liked having them very much."

We came back. We brought them back to town and when we got there it was evening.—The lady who was taking me around said, "I believe you will have to sleep for a while. You can't stay at the depot because it is too cold." So we stayed and slept at the hotel. I told the woman at the hotel desk to wake us up in time and she did so—. We headed for the depot and when the train arrived we boarded it. Then we travelled for a day and a night and we came to St. Paul. We changed trains and then we got home. We got off at Merrillan and there we took a taxi that brought us home.

The little grandchildren lived at my house. They went to school and they stayed there with me and they grew big. When they reached school age they went to school.

Then I finally located my daughter. We used to write letters to each other. Eventually when the older girl became an adolescent, I did not want her to grow up there. I did not want her to be at the mission so I said to her that she was to go back to her mother. She was very happy. I told my daughter that I was going to send back the older girl and younger boy. She was very thankful. She even sent the money for their fare. She sent them one hundred dollars. So they went back to their mother who was in California.

After two years the older boy went back too. He was big by then, almost a man, and I had kept him and the baby.[19] The younger girl is the only one I kept and she is the only one I have with me today. Maybe I will send her back too. I am getting old to be caring for children.[20]

My children always want to take me home with them, but I never accepted their offers.[21] I always say, "Not until I am much older. When I am so old that I cannot care for myself, then you can take care of me." All of my children are very willing to take care of me, but I like to live by myself. I go visiting here and there. Sometimes I go to Nebraska and see my relatives.

Once when I came back from Nebraska one of my relatives had died. His name was Fish Back, Mitchell Redcloud, Sr. He had three sons. One time he had told me a young white girl was going to come to Black River Falls and that she was his daughter. He even gave her a Winnebago name. Therefore, she was my niece. All of our relatives liked her very much. That is how it was. She thought a lot of us too and she liked Indians. She was an only child. When the Indians talked about their affairs, whatever they knew, she knew more. She helped the Indians. Whatever happened long ago, wherever they settled, she found out all about it and then she helped the Indians.[22]

She wanted me to do her a favor. "Auntie," she said, "if

you come and visit me we will write down Indian stories in a book.'' That is why I am here, saying this at her home. I even rode in an airplane, and I came here. And here I am, telling in Winnebago how I lived my life. This I have written.

❧ APPENDIX A

FIRST VERSION OF MOUNTAIN WOLF
WOMAN'S AUTOBIOGRAPHY [1]

Mother had me, they said, at East Fort Creek. Our grandfather lived there. He was called Náqijohnga, John The Fourth Son. They were making maple sugar while they were living there. There mother had me, and I was the very last child. "Poor quality," they used to say of the last child.

Again, we used to live at Black River Falls in a house made of logs. We all used to live there. When that log house was newly made, mother said that I walked there for the first time. Mother said that before I began walking she and my sister White Thunder, before my sister was married, apparently had gone to town and were evidently returning across a river called Levis Creek. That was before there was a bridge to cross over and before there was a road where they walked along. I was evidently tired so mother carried me on her back and my older sister carried the empty cradleboard as we returned. There was water down there and we waded across it. My sister held her skirt up just so far that it would not get wet. The creek below was very swift and there where they waded as they were crossing, my mother carried me and my sister carried the cradle.

Probably because I was frightened I remembered a woman walking along ahead of me carrying an empty cradle. I know that we did not cross again a second time [i.e., that she recollects this specific incident]. Eventually, when I was big, I asked my mother about it. "Mother," I said, "one time long past I saw that." She replied, "Do you remember? That was your sister walking along carrying your empty cradle. You probably remember because you were scared," she said. Then again, I forgot.

At one time before there were white people across from Black River Falls, only a great many Indians lived there. That was very fine land there when the Indians camped at that place in the springtime in order to catch fish. They speared fish and father did that too. They called those fish sturgeon. Father speared a great big one that was as big as a man. Father carried it on his back and its tail even dragged on the ground. He brought it home and it was lying there on the ground, its belly distended. Turned over on its side, that fish was lying there almost like a man with a big belly. I was probably surprised by that creature that I remembered it. Again, I asked my mother about it. I said, "I saw that once."

She said, "You were but two years old. Did you remember that?" "Yes," I said.

To continue, while we were living there, I got lost. At that place the Black River lies at the foot of very high, steep banks. The people thought I might have fallen down the bank and they looked for me. They all looked and looked. There was an old lady there who could foretell things so they gave her tobacco to see what would become of me. Then someone returned from town nearby and they said to him, "Little Siga is lost."

"Oh," he said, "her father is leading her by the hand all around the town."

It seems that father had gone to town. On the way, there was a cow that was probably tethered there and I was frightened by that cow. Father did not know that I was following along behind him. Evidently in fear of that cow, I began to cry. Father led me by the hand. He went to town taking me with him. In time we returned and so they had me back alive.

After a while we went back to the log house where we usually lived and mother and father planted a garden. There were many Indian people living all around there. To the south was Maxaǵega [meaning unknown] whom they called Black Hawk. The river goes through there and he lived by the water. His sister lived beside him. Another Black Hawk lived there too. Those siblings lived there. That was very long ago. East of there was Young Swan and then a sixth son they called Old Eats A Lot. They all lived near each other in nice frame houses. They used to live there very comfortably.

East of there lived Little Gray and then King Of Thunder and then Jumping Up. I don't know why they called him that. More people lived east of there. Southeast there were also houses and just east of where we lived was Raccoon Skin Cap. Our father's aunt and our oldest grandmother lived there. That was somewhat north where our oldest grandmother and her younger sister stayed. Nearby was mother's sister Queen Of Thunder. Then there was one they called Wind Blow. He used to live in a nice frame house.

Then farther east were Lightning and a Black Hawk. They were brothers. Across the river was Antlers, a big old man, and his wife whom they called Duck. Close by was Yellow Thunder Woman and her husband they called Tall Fourth Son; he was a tall, skinny old man. We used to be afraid of him, that big old man. He was a poisoner. Then there was Striking Thunder and his wife who was called White Woman. They used to live there and then downstream was Strikes The Tree and his wife. The people would often dance there where a big feast lodge stood. They held many dances and feasts.

They call it the sore eye dance. They used to say, "At night we are going to do that" [i.e., perform the dance]. That was a holy dance they used to say. Whoever was sick would become well, father used to say. Two women danced in front, they used to have women lead the dance. They held war dances there too.

Farther on there lived other people. One was called Bear Den. Many people used to live there long ago when I was small. I used to see them. There was Handles Lightning and his wife Glory Of The Morning. Then there was a woman called Nojiiŋga, Strikes The Tree, and her mother, an old lady, who stayed there, and her brother Bites The Deer. They all used to live there. Another one they called Hurt Leg, probably he was lame. Then there was father's brother and his wife, a Bear Clan woman. They used to call her Little Wíhanga. I think her name was Searching, that was her Bear Clan name. Below the hill at the edge of the Black River was an old lady they called Blue Eyes, she was the mother of Earth Woman. Then nearby was Shining Man. Next came Flying Low who had a lot of grown-up daughters all living there together.

Long ago they used to live wherever the elders stayed. They got along together harmoniously. None of them was at odds with another. In the beginning people loved each other. They even would all live in one house, never disagreeing. We too used to live this way, my three brothers, Crashing Thunder, Lightning Strikes About, and Big Winnebago, and my sisters. The oldest sister was called White Thunder, next was Bald Eagle. The third daughter died, mother said. Next was the fourth daughter and then myself.

We were never at odds with one another, nor quarrelling nor scolding one another. Mother and father never scolded any of us, however, we were probably well behaved. They never used to scold me. Now children are not like that. They are even against their own parents. But my children were never against me. I have six daughters and two sons. My own children are big now. They would never say, "shut up"[2] to me, none of them were ever against me. They all live here and there. I like it that way. At first I used to be lonesome, but I got over it. They are doing well and I am getting along well. My children live here and there and I can visit them. They come and call for me. That is how it is today.

When I was a little girl I went to school when I was nine years old. They let me go to school. My oldest brother said I should go to school. He said he liked to hear women speak English. They let me attend school at Tomah for two years and then I went to school at Wittenberg. Then I knew many things but not much any more. I did not even finish the sixth grade. It was in the spring before school was out that they made me stop attending school. I went there when I was thirteen years old. There I became a Christian, Lutheran they called that kind of Christian. They baptized me and confirmed me and since then I am a Christian. They made me stop going to school in order to have a husband.

I even cried. Mother combed my hair. She dressed me in my little clothes, telling me, "Your brothers say you are to do this. If you do not do it, you are going to make them ashamed. I think they have been sitting around drinking but you will have to do it," mother said.

My brother used to drink and it was probably when brother Hágaga was drinking that they arranged for me to marry that man. He sat there using his hat to fan the mosquitoes from my brother. My brother realized this when he awoke in the morning. He took pity on that man sitting there. Brother was thinking to himself, "I have many sisters, that must be why he is doing this for me." Thus they gave me away. They wanted me to marry that man.

My father said, "You do not have very many things to wear." I had a pet pony, a three year old dapple gray. He said, "I have brought your horse for you. You will go riding, you will not walk." Then that man led. He set off and I followed. We came to a bank. There he too mounted the horse and we both rode back together. We went back where I was led. Thus I became a daughter-in-law. It was the son of a man called Pine that they made me marry. We returned to where they lived and there were women sitting there. All of his female relatives were sitting there.

Upon my arrival I took off all of the things I was wearing. I put them down and his mother came and took them. I had worn a blanket-shawl skirt and I had another one. Then I wore little things, jewelry that they took for themselves. Each one took something for herself and contributed something.

After while in about three or four days they let me go back with four horses and a double shawl so full of things they could barely tie the corners together. That much they gave me to bring back. Afterwards they gave me two more horses. Six horses they gave me when I married my husband.

However, that first time when I went away, mother said to me when I cried, "My dear little girl, I value you greatly but there is nothing to be done. You must do this. Eventually when you are older you can make all of your own decisions. You can marry any man whom you think you want." That is what she said to me. I would never forget that!

I had two children and then I left this man. He was a jealous kind of man, even jealous and making accusations about close relatives. I finally left him.

Then there was another man. I did not care much for this one but I married him. They made accusations about this man and me. They spoke of me as a dark woman. Finally I said, "Sometimes men like dark women." I laughed. The man kept talking with me, trying to make me marry him. But I didn't want to. His wife was jealous and that is why she said that [calling Mountain Wolf Woman a dark woman]. Then my brother Crashing Thunder told me to do so, and so that is why I married this man. I married him and she gave him up. He said, "Let us go immediately and get a marriage license so that she will not bother us." We went there to the courthouse at Black River Falls and got a marriage license. However, this woman used to come around where I was but after while we went our own way.

After we went to Nebraska we ate peyote. I was there in Nebraska for sixteen years. This man used to plant a garden. He rented a farm and there we used to live. After while we had children. My older sister, that big woman,[3] the fourth daughter, said that she would rear my children for me. She had no children and she would raise the children that I already had, my first and second daughters. She raised them very well. Then I had some other children.[4] Three of my children died, the two older boys and the fourth daughter. But today my children are all grown up and they live here and there.

Oh, there is something that I did not tell you. When I was a daughter-in-law back there at the Pine household, one of my brothers died. They were going to let me take his place in the medicine lodge. However, then my mother-in-law had me make clothing. I used to sew clothing and I did not even know that I was doing this for myself. After while they held a medicine dance. They told us we should sit there. I wondered why they were saying this for no reason. At first only a few were sitting there.[5] There my mother-in-law said to me, "Daughter-in-law, people make this way. This is so that you and your little children may live here with the people in harmony. This is holy. My mother valued this way. I have always thought it would be very good for the one who takes that sitting place. Daughter-in-law, this is my way. You will be a leader.[6] This way is the one mother liked. In this way we people are going to live. You are going to be taken care of in this way. It is a good way for people to live," she said to me.

I had not even been thinking about that. I did not know that they would let me make medicine.[7] Thus I joined the medicine lodge. I was once a Christian. Then, when we went to Nebraska I ate peyote which is even a Christian way. Three things I did. But peyote alone is the best. I learned very many things.

Whatever is good, that I would do. Whatever is good to say, that I would say. These people are good to live with. I was respected among these people. I moved towards a good way. I thought that was a good thing, that I would be strengthened. That is the way I am. I pray to God. I always ask of him that I move towards a good way, that my children and my grandchildren and the people live well. I was strengthened. Today I am in good health. I continue to live happily. I pray for the sick. I pray for the dead. Whatever good I can say, that I say. That is the way I always try to be. If anyone says anything to me, I always say good of him, then nothing he is saying can hurt me. That is what I do. That is the way I am.

I am old, but though I am seventy-three years old my body is strong. I make my own clothing. There are women living here and there today who are younger than I am who are helplessly infirm. I am able to move about. Where I live I care for myself. My children sometimes say they would take care of me. "Wait a while," I say, "until I am older. You can take care of me when I can no longer take care of myself." I always say I am happy the way I am and that I hope to continue in that fashion. If I am good to people, after while, when my life ends, I expect to go to heaven.[8] I say no more.

✿ APPENDIX B

COMMENTARY BY NANCY OESTREICH LURIE

While Mountain Wolf Woman and I were still transcribing the Winnebago version of her story, Paul Radin graciously consented to make the journey from his home in Massachusetts to Michigan to observe our progress and plan for the final preparation of the manuscript. He had been greatly interested in the project from its inception and had been instrumental in obtaining the grant from the Bollingen Foundation by which it was in part financed. Dr. Radin was to have written an extended commentary comparing the autobiographies of Crashing Thunder and Mountain Wolf Woman, but his death in February of 1959 deprived us of the benefit of his observations. The task now falls to me and while an inadequate substitute, I am able to draw in part on observations and information he provided during the course of his visit in Ann Arbor.

Paul Radin sensed from what he knew personally and had heard about Crashing Thunder that in this man's story lay a dramatic and psychologically intriguing record. However, Crashing Thunder was reluctant to give his story, and only agreed when the fee offered by Radin could relieve the financial difficulties in which he found himself at the time. Having given his word, Crashing Thunder set about his work with intense concentration, and in the course of two sessions of protracted effort, wrote the autobiography. He wrote the

story in the Winnebago syllabary script and Radin did not
see the manuscript until it was completed. Radin then translated it, aided mainly by an educated Winnebago named
Oliver La Mere, and assisted by Crashing Thunder and his
older brother.

Other data obtained at different times primarily from
Crashing Thunder were incorporated into the text. Those sections written in the first person singular are from the original
manuscript, whereas accounts of mythology and descriptions
of Winnebago culture of a more general nature are from
Radin's field notes. The manuscript was first published by the
University of California in 1920,[1] and was published in 1926
in somewhat revised form as *Crashing Thunder*.[2] Unless otherwise noted, all page references in the following commentary
will be to the later edition.

As stated in the preface of the present work, Mountain
Wolf Woman agreed to let me publish her autobiography because the request was made in terms of our aunt-niece relationship. She expected remuneration but as a reciprocal gift
rather than as payment for her work. Thus, an element of
coercion was involved with both Crashing Thunder and Mountain Wolf Woman; Radin took advantage of his informant's
poverty and I manipulated the kinship structure for my own
purposes. However, while neither informant would have written an autobiography without the stimulus provided by an
anthropologist, both informants were chosen because it was
possible to interest them in the work and they were eminently
qualified to perform the task.

Radin found it necessary to add material to the original
autobiography as noted. This was not the case with Mountain
Wolf Woman's story, except for clarification of specific
phrases, largely because of the technological advantage of the
tape recorder. While I did far less editing than Radin, those

93

sections of Crashing Thunder's autobiography originally written in his own hand are purely his own work. Mountain Wolf Woman told her story to me and though I could not always follow what she was saying in Winnebago, I was still an audience and she was alert to my responses.

I endeavored not to influence Mountain Wolf Woman except to provide supportive interest in anything she might choose to discuss. During the course of ordinary conversation she often mentioned incidents, inquiring if they ought to be included. I always said they should be recorded. In two instances she told of occurrences which she did not want incorporated in the narrative and I must respect her confidence in this regard. She feared they would sound boastful and cause her to be ridiculed.

We worked at a far more leisurely pace than had Crashing Thunder, devoting about four hours each day to the project and stopping whenever Mountain Wolf Woman felt fatigued or wanted to think about a topic she wished to discuss. After Mountain Wolf Woman completed her story in Winnebago, she repeated it in English. She was understandably too weary by then to undertake a word by word translation, but her English version is remarkably parallel to the Winnebago account. I am indebted in this regard to Gertrude P. Kurath (Mrs. Hans Kurath) of Ann Arbor for the loan of her tape recorder, which expedited this phase of the work, enabling me to play an episode from the Winnebago tapes on her machine and immediately record Mountain Wolf Woman's translation with my machine.

As Mountain Wolf Woman listened to the Winnebago tapes, she was reminded of further incidents she wished to include and asked that I keep a list of these. A final set of tapes was accordingly transcribed in both Winnebago and English. Mountain Wolf Woman indicated at which points in the final manuscript these incidents should be inserted.

I had intended to translate the Winnebago account into literary English with no further help, but soon found I was not equal to the task. Fortunately, I was able to obtain the services of a grandniece of Mountain Wolf Woman, Frances Thundercloud Wentz (Mrs. Roger Wentz), in making a detailed translation. I cannot express adequately the extent of my gratitude to Mrs. Wentz for her patience, interest in the task, objectivity, and awareness of items of special cultural significance. Later, I checked the final manuscript with Mountain Wolf Woman. The work with Mrs. Wentz and the discussions with Mountain Wolf Woman were conducted for several weeks during the spring and fall of 1958 and the early winter of 1959 in Milwaukee, Wisconsin, at the home of my mother, Rayline D. Oestreich (Mrs. Carl R. Oestreich). I wish to take this opportunity to extend my thanks to my mother for her generosity and hospitality in helping to bring the project to completion.

The final preparation of an acceptable English narrative from a literary and scholarly point of view required decisions for which I must take full responsibility: choice of tenses, equivalents of idiomatic expressions, insertion of words necessary for clarification and the like. Mountain Wolf Woman is an accomplished mimic, often quoting exchanges of conversation by changing the tone of her voice to indicate the various speakers. In some cases I have supplied such terms as "he said," "I said," etc., without noting such editing on my part. Likewise, as we progressed from one recording session to the next, Mountain Wolf Woman often repeated phrases from the foregoing session in order to orient herself. I have simply deleted these repetitions. The most extensive reworking of Mountain Wolf Woman's narrative concerned the use of English names (see Chapter VI, note 5).

A conscious effort was made to conform closely to the Winnebago wording rather than to paraphrase in a more con-

95

ventional English style. An inevitable degree of distortion occurs in any translation, but I was guided by Radin's technique in the translation of *Crashing Thunder* so that the distortion is at least standardized at what I consider a minimal level if the two volumes are to be used comparatively.

In cases where different nuances of meaning occurred in the alternative translations given by Mountain Wolf Woman and Mrs. Wentz, I was guided by Mountain Wolf Woman's choices as probably truer reflections of her personal conception of such matters. In some instances, however, Mrs. Wentz's excellent command of English and remarkable vocabulary provided greater fidelity to the literary beauty and effectiveness of the Winnebago version than did Mountain Wolf Woman with her more limited English.

I would like to express a final note of thanks to the persons and organizations responsible for the illustrative materials included in this publication. The photographs for which no citations are given come from a collection housed at the Black River Falls Public Library and include pictures taken by two early professional photographers of the town, C. J. van Schaik and A. J. Roiselands, as well as pictures collected by Miss Emma Gebhardt. Mrs. Frances Perry, librarian of the Black River Falls Public Library who is in charge of the photographic collection, gave most generously of her time, personal interest and knowledge in helping me select the photographs used in this book. Mountain Wolf Woman also spent several days with us looking through the pictures and identifying people and dates. Funds for the trip to Black River Falls were supplied by The University of Michigan Research Institute.

Specific comparisons of the autobiographies of Mountain Wolf Woman and Crashing Thunder have been made in the notes following each chapter. However, there are certain general considerations which require further discussion. A major difficulty arises from the fact that Crashing Thunder is not the true name of the writer of the autobiography published by Radin in 1926. It is actually the name of his oldest sibling whose autobiography was Radin's first publication of a life history.[3] Alias Crashing Thunder was really named Big Winnebago. According to Mountain Wolf Woman, this curious name was bestowed by his maternal grandmother, an unusual but not unheard of variation on the traditional pattern of naming children after the paternal clan. The grandmother was one of the last representatives of a family line which claimed to be of pure Winnebago descent. Although her own children and grandchildren were of mixed descent, she wished to commemorate the fact of her ancestry in the name of at least one grandson.

Radin had several reasons for giving his author a nom de plume and for choosing the name Crashing Thunder. It was Radin's opinion, with which I am strongly inclined to agree, that while the name hoćáŋkxátega is impressive enough, when it is rendered into literal English as "Big Winnebago," there is something amusingly inappropriate about it. As the title of a book it is somehow evocative of the "heap big Indian" school of fiction writing. Crashing Thunder is infinitely more dramatic and at the same time more typical of Winnebago clan names.

Big Winnebago was, furthermore, not eager to be identified as the author of the autobiography. In the 1920 edition, Radin refers to him as S.B., the initials of his English name. By 1926 the real Crashing Thunder had died and since he had been an even more important informant than Big Winnebago, and a considerably less controversial figure, Radin calculated that a book by Crashing Thunder would not evoke undue curiosity among the Winnebago generally. Big Winnebago was worried lest he be accused of being a braggart in thinking his life so important that he set it forth in a book for white people. To a Winnebago this is a very real problem and one which Mountain Wolf Woman avoids by the fact that her narrative is published to oblige a niece.

Even Big Winnebago tried to use this technique by imputing kinship to Radin: "Then my brother had us do this work . . ." (1920, 449). For reasons I cannot explain, Radin deleted this phrase in the 1926 edition (p. 203). Although Radin protected the identity of his informant in the title of the book, he provided a clue for later scholarly investigators. In the account of the killing of a Potawatomi, the author says, "I . . . counted coup first, and announced my new name, ... *Big Winnebago*" (p. 150). Although "new" is not an exact translation of the text, it conforms to traditional Winnebago practice in the taking of a new name upon performing a warlike deed.

Now that Big Winnebago has outlived most of his peers, he regrets that his work and fame are attributed to his brother. However, as late as 1944, when I mentioned the name to an elderly Winnebago whose apparent age suggested he might be a contemporary of Radin's famous informant, he told me simply, "Crashing Thunder was my brother." Later I learned I had been talking to Big Winnebago who had long ago taken a new English surname. I had had no clue to his identity in the initials, S.B. He had known perfectly well that I was interested in the writer of the autobiography published in 1926.

Mountain Wolf Woman refers frequently to both of the brothers in her autobiography, speaking of them according to their true names. With the exception of the sister nearest her in age, Big Winnebago is the sibling mentioned most often in Mountain Wolf Woman's story. This is fortunate for purposes of comparing the two accounts, but it is probably due more to Big Winnebago's longevity than to any particular distinctiveness of his personality as it affected Mountain Wolf Woman. Of all her siblings she most admired her oldest brother, the real Crashing Thunder. However, since the name Crashing Thunder is so firmly established in the anthropological literature, I will continue to use it in the following observations to refer to the writer of the autobiography published in 1926.

Crashing Thunder described Mountain Wolf Woman as ". . . my youngest sister, the one to whom we all listened most attentively" (p. 170). He did not always heed her advice nor did his actions always meet with her approval, but he was perfectly sincere in acknowledging that his youngest sibling enjoyed the esteem of her family for her intelligence, good nature and strength of character. But where Mountain Wolf Woman speaks at length of her siblings, Crashing Thunder mentions Mountain Wolf Woman only once, some of his siblings not at all. Crashing Thunder's need for personal recognition and ego gratification stands in sharp contrast to Mountain Wolf Woman's security in this regard. He begins his autobiography with the account of a family prophecy concerning his birth, that his mother ". . . was about to bear a child who will not be an ordinary individual" (p. 1). Mountain Wolf Woman, after listing all of her siblings, notes her status as the youngest one in the family by recalling an old Winnebago joke about the alleged nature of the last child: waihak, "poor quality."

In fairness to Crashing Thunder it should be noted that he wrote his autobiography before he was forty-five years old, whereas Mountain Wolf Woman doubtless derives some measure of her self-assurance from being over seventy in a culture which still tends to esteem the aged. Possibly her admitted status in childhood as the petted baby in the family contributed significantly to the formation of her personality in comparison to the different experiences of Crashing Thunder as the fifth of eight children.

Aside from these factors of age and sibling rank, I believe that the basic difference in personality represented in the autobiographies of Crashing Thunder and Mountain Wolf Woman is a fundamental difference between males and females generally among the Winnebago. In large part, Mountain Wolf Woman's autobiography is a predictable reflection of the greater self-confidence enjoyed by women in comparison to men in a culture undergoing rapid and destructive changes. As was true of many American Indian groups, the roles of wife, mother and homemaker for which the Winnebago girl was prepared could be fulfilled in adulthood despite the vagaries of acculturation. There is another dimension that might be considered as well. Even in aboriginal times and on through the late historic period, warfare meant men would be absent for varying times and necessitated a degree of self-reliance among Winnebago women. Later, despite the terrible disruption of domestic life because of government removals and resettlement on a series of reservations, women still had to care for children, prepare meals, mend clothing and carry out other familiar tasks as a matter of survival.

Winnebago boys were prepared for traditional roles as warriors, hunters and shamans long after these roles stood little chance of effective fulfillment. For example, Crashing Thunder sought to be a respected warrior by taking part in the killing of a Potawatomi Indian. His father understood and appreciated his motives, but in the opinion of white officialdom he was an accomplice in a pointless murder (pp. 148–67).

The sense of personal adequacy displayed by Mountain

Wolf Woman can be attributed to more than the greater continuity and stability of female roles. Cultural change has indeed affected the lives of Winnebago women, but in contrast to men, they have benefited by the change to some extent. Their socially humbler roles have acquired greater economic power at the expense of the more prestigious male roles. Traditionally, the Winnebago male provided game, the primary subsistence item of the group as well as the main source of clothing. This continued to be the case during the long period of the fur trade when even the peltry animals trapped by men brought new wealth in material goods to the Winnebago. Women raised garden produce and gathered wild foods, and though they contributed significantly to the family larder their offerings were not held in the high esteem accorded venison or bear meat.

Within the lifetime of Mountain Wolf Woman's oldest sibling it became extremely difficult to subsist by hunting and gardening. White settlers began to occupy the lands of the Winnebago and the tribe was driven from its homeland. Trapping became ever less profitable while the Winnebago became increasingly more dependent on the trader's stock as necessary to their existence. When they became involved in a cash economy, the Winnebago cast about for new sources of subsistence. They found a solution to their economic problems in harvesting fruit and vegetable crops for white employers or selling wild vegetable produce to white people. Although both men and women engaged in these tasks, gathering and agricultural activities were matters with which women were identified and in which they traditionally excelled.

Finally, the tourist trade of the last sixty years has become exceptionally important to the Winnebago and has given women an added source of income in the production of beadwork and basketry. Although basketry is a relatively new

101

craft learned from more easterly tribes, it has on occasion been the mainstay of many Winnebago families. Mountain Wolf Woman takes her productive activities so much for granted that she does not even mention that during most of her adult life and throughout her wide travels and changes of residence she has made baskets to obtain cash. She implies that men are the providers and speaks approvingly of her second husband as industrious. In plain fact, she has always contributed a large amount to the family income and furthermore exercised primary control over family finances.

Mountain Wolf Woman is a practical person. Her story lacks the emotional intensity of personal crises, indecision and violence found in her brother's autobiography. Though interlarded with general descriptions of Winnebago customs, the theme of Crashing Thunder's personal story is the seeking of a satisfactory way of life on the part of an ambitious but frustrated individual. He finds it ultimately in the value system of the peyote religion. Mountain Wolf Woman's narrative is primarily the story of the Winnebago over the last seventy-five years. She devotes attention to matters that concerned her family and the entire Winnebago tribe before her birth, and she ends her story with an account of her children, grandchildren and great-grandchildren. They will continue the story of the Winnebago long after she is gone.

The significance of peyote in the two autobiographies illustrates the fundamental difference in outlook of Crashing Thunder and Mountain Wolf Woman. Crashing Thunder, given to intellectualizing, was attracted and yet repelled by this new and curious religion. He actually turned to Mountain Wolf Woman for advice on the subject (p. 170). She advised him against eating peyote. In earlier field work with Mountain Wolf Woman she once told me that she had heard bad things about peyote and had been afraid of it. She was willing to try peyote, however, when her sister told her that it might ease the pains of childbirth. Satisfied that it was efficacious for this purpose, she accepted it as a good thing and began to attend peyote meetings.

The strong moralistic interests of the early peyotists merely reinforced opinions to which she already subscribed. Unlike her brother who became concerned about salvation after a series of frightening peyote visions convinced him that he was damned unless he changed his ways, Mountain Wolf Woman saw herself as an angel and was assured that she would go to heaven. This is not to disparage the importance of peyote for Mountain Wolf Woman, but her conviction that it is a "true" religion is characteristically uncomplicated. She *saw* Jesus. In the medicine lodge and the white Christian churches they just talk about God.

Although Mountain Wolf Woman is exceptionally outgoing compared to the Winnebago as a group, characteristic and recurrent Winnebago themes underlie her opinions, decisions, and behavior. Many of these themes have been observed among other Indian groups, particularly the Ojibwa, but often distinctively Winnebago shadings are given to the expression of these themes.

Notable and of widespread occurrence among American Indians is an extreme practicality coupled with a strong emphasis on immediacy. Events tend to be treated as discrete entities and distaste is felt for projects which involve long range planning. We find this well illustrated in Mountain Wolf Woman's opinion of farming. However, farming was not abandoned until it had been given a fair and successful trial. My personal feeling is that the Winnebago are not so much easily discouraged as easily bored. They expect variety of experience as the nature of the universe and seek varied tasks almost in the sense of educational opportunities.

This, of course, relates to another widespread theme among American Indians, adaptability and self-reliance. The Winnebago often say, "I like to be my own boss." For this reason they like wage work and piecework because they feel free to quit whenever they like. A mere employer can never be a master. What they dread is enslavement to capital investments. This picture is changing and some of the younger Winnebago as well as a few individuals of Mountain Wolf Woman's generation have shown remarkable aptitude for entrepreneurial enterprise. However, Mountain Wolf Woman is more typical of the Winnebago considered generally when she says, "Whatever the circumstances, the Indian is always doing something useful."

A complex of related themes regarding interpersonal relations may be noted in the stories of both Crashing Thunder and Mountain Wolf Woman. The familiar matters of hostility, aggression and social control of aggression are involved. The Winnebago go out of their way to avoid expressing aggression directly, either physically or verbally. It is therefore not surprising that we find frequent mention of gossip and witchcraft in the two autobiographies. Gossip is not directed at a person, it simply gets back to him to have its desired effect. Witchcraft is accomplished by stealth and the witch tries to conceal his identity. The Winnebago also go out of their way to avoid situations which might simply be unpleasant in terms of making them feel uncomfortable, foolish or mildly anxious. Recourse is often had to the hasty and unexplained departure. Since relations with whites are very apt to be fraught with anxiety, it is understandable that most of the instances of flight recounted by Mountain Wolf Woman and Crashing Thunder concern situations involving whites.

Crashing Thunder provides a particularly telling example (pp. 143–44). He was known as a troublemaker and when he and a companion got into a drunken brawl with some local whites, a whole group of Indians with whom he had been visiting simply stole away in the night. Crashing Thunder says, ''These poor people were really trying to get away from us for they thought that the white people would really follow us and fight.''

In effect, the group was both avoiding difficulties and ostracizing Crashing Thunder and his friend. Ostracism is a powerful social control and takes various forms. A common technique is to express disapproval by maintaining an oppressive silence and an utterly blank face. I have seen obstreperous drunks forced away from a disapproving gathering so effectively by this method that they seemed almost to question their own existence as they slunk off puzzled and defeated.

While this system of withdrawal is directed outward, it is also indicative of self-repression on the part of the person who employs it. Physically violent expressions of hostility do occur but can almost always be traced to liquor having dissolved customary reserve. The sometimes incredible excesses of drunken aggression may be an indication of the excessive degree of sober repression. I am inclined to believe that this is often misplaced aggression but since I am not qualified to speak as a social psychologist I can only point to the fact that in Nebraska there is more violent drunkenness and a far less happy socioeconomic relation to whites than is the case in Wisconsin.

In relations with white people generally, the Winnebago tend to maintain a diffident and serious appearance until they know the white person as a friend. The Winnebago usually indicate that this stage is reached by engaging in good-natured teasing of the white person. Mountain Wolf Woman is exceptional in this regard in that she makes friends with strange white people readily and will even initiate conversations. I was often struck by the contrast she presented to her sister whom I also knew well. The sister, Hinákega, spoke virtually no English but even among Winnebago people her demeanor was more reserved than that of Mountain Wolf Woman. Even acculturated young Winnebago are apt to go into a blank-faced withdrawal if approached by strange whites in what they consider too familiar terms. However, Mountain Wolf Woman is typical of the Winnebago in recognizing categories of whites on the basis of class and personal character. It is the unusual Winnebago who considers all whites bad or hostile.

On the basis of my brief but always cordial contacts with Crashing Thunder and perhaps because of my initial meeting with him, I am inclined to think that his behavior toward whites more closely conforms to the Winnebago norm. He is pleasant and courteous, and on the basis of work with a number of anthropologists as well as employment in tourist attractions such as the Wisconsin Dells Indian ceremonial, he is even sophisticated about the ways of the white world. However, I always have an impression of dignified and even somewhat distant formality which reminds me more of his sister Hinákega than Mountain Wolf Woman.

Professor Milton Barnett of the Anthropology Department of the University of Wisconsin has been working with Crashing Thunder for the past several years. His work is intended to bring the original autobiography up to date as well as to uncover Crashing Thunder's retrospect opinions about matters discussed in it. The publication of this study will round out an exceptionally interesting series of life histories in a single tribe: the original autobiography, the brief narrative of the true Crashing Thunder, and the present volume.

And now the story is truly ended. Mountain Wolf Woman died quietly in her sleep the morning of November 9, 1960,

the very day that I also received notification that the galleys
of her narrative were ready for me to proofread. Thus, it is
possible to add this final commentary while my descriptive
notes concerning Mountain Wolf Woman remain in the present
tense.

Mountain Wolf Woman had returned to her home at Black
River Falls after a visit at the home of one of her children. She
apparently caught cold in the course of sealing windows and
otherwise preparing her house for the winter. At her request,
neighbors drove her to the clinic at Black River Falls where her
condition was diagnosed as pleurisy and pneumonia. After a
week's stay at the clinic she appeared to be recovering and
told visitors that she intended to go home on November 9. However, when I went to Black River Falls for the funeral, I
learned that she had told one close relative that she did not
want to worry her children, but that she really meant she was
going to her spiritual home. Whether or not this is apocryphal
is unimportant; it is in keeping with Winnebago expectation
that people who are good and wise and old are privileged to
foretell their own deaths. After all, Mountain Wolf Woman
reported just such a prophecy from her own husband.

The funeral arrangements reflected the varying religious
affiliations among the Winnebago. Conservative relatives and
friends held a brief version of the traditional Winnebago wake
at a community some distance from Black River Falls; her own
peyote beliefs were represented in a well-attended peyote meeting held at her home the night before her burial; and on Saturday, November 12, 1960, she was laid to rest at the mission
cemetery at Black River Falls after Christian services at the
mission church.

Many Winnebago are understandably distressed by the
apparent evidence of religious confusion in the holding of two
or more different kinds of rituals when a Winnebago dies.
Nevertheless, when I saw the several hundred people gathered

from near and far to pay their last respects, my own feeling was that the three rituals were somehow fitting and proper. Mountain Wolf Woman's own life had included participation in all three religions and while she considered herself a peyotist, she retained virtues of generosity and obligation to kindred of her traditionally Winnebago childhood. She accepted Christianity in her baptism and confirmation at a mission boarding school. Finally, she found in the peyote religion a deep sense of spiritual understanding and experience. Her many friends and relatives in these different religious groups all desired most earnestly to express their grief in their loss and their respect for her memory in the way each found most meaningful.

✀ APPENDIX C

For readers unfamiliar with linguistic orthography the following list may prove helpful. All consonants are pronounced as in English except for the following:

c — ch

š — sh

r — a flap, that is a single trill of *r* sound

ŋ — in effect, a nasalization of the preceding vowel, similar to *n* sound in English word *wing*

x — There is nothing comparable to this and the following sound in English. Some writers liken it to the harsh *ch* sound in certain German dialects in such words as *ich*.

q — This sound is the same as the above except that it is voiced and usually produced somewhat farther back in the throat.

Vowels are pronounced as follows:

a — as in English *father*

e — as in English *mate*

i — as in English *me*

o — as in English *go*

u — as in English *boot*

ω — as in English *put*

ʌ — as in English *but*

i — as in English *pit*

ε — as in English *met*

The vowel sounds are approximations to English sounds since there are regional variations in English pronunciations of these sounds. In linguistic terms, the orthography used is phonemic rather than phonetic and does not indicate the range of *k* sounds for example, which vary widely with consonantal and vowel environment. Likewise, the exceedingly complex problems of vowel length, as related to stress, and vowel duplication have not been dealt with. All initial vowels are given a slight glottal treatment, as in English, so only the occurrence of full glottal stops (ˀ) is noted.

✻ NOTES TO CHAPTER I

1. Mountain Wolf Woman knows that she was born in April 1884, but the exact day is unknown.
2. Recollection of incidents occurring as early as a child's second year is considered a sign of extraordinary intelligence, and in telling of this situation, Mountain Wolf Woman mimicked the surprised tone of her mother's voice.
3. Traditionally, each Winnebago had two names, a sex-birth order name and a formal, ceremonial name usually derived from his clan affiliation. Mountain Wolf Woman omits the sex-birth order names of the first two children, which would be Hínuga for the first daughter and Kúnuga for the first son. Her parents had only three sons, and so the fourth name for a boy, Náqiga, is not given. After the fourth son, succeeding boys' names are diminutive forms of Náqiga, but succeeding girls' names after the fourth daughter are diminutive forms of Haksigaga, the third girl's name. Thus, Mountain Wolf Woman's sex-birth order name is Haksigaxunuga but she was usually called Haksigaxunuñiŋka or Little Fifth Daughter to indicate her small size. The (ga) ending, changing to (ka) after (k), is the referent form. The listing is begun again with each set of children by a different spouse. Thus, Mountain Wolf Woman has two daughters named Hínuga and two daughters named Wíhaŋga because they have different fathers.

   During the lifetime of Mountain Wolf Woman's father the Winnebago began to acquire surnames as government enrollments were made of the tribe. Usually these were translations of an individual's Indian name or nickname, but sometimes Winnebago took the surnames of white acquaintances. By the time Mountain Wolf Woman was a child, surnames were established for her generation, but many older people in the narrative were never known by any except their Winnebago names. Also,

English first names were bestowed at the time of enrollments and became increasingly popular, so that all of Mountain Wolf Woman's contemporaries have English first names and surnames.

4. Among the Winnebago old people are frequently suspect as witches since it is believed that longevity may be achieved by killing people, particularly relatives, by means of magic medicines. The witch thus acquires the unfulfilled life span of the deceased. The aged are therefore indulged because their envy may lead to revenge. However, the ideal reason given for respecting the aged is that they are wise due to long experience and almost sacred because of their closeness to death and the spirit world, and can thus bestow blessings upon people they like. Longevity results, ideally, from having lived a good life and having acquired blessings from spirits or people able to give the gift of longevity, or from following the tenets of the medicine lodge. A final note should be made about referring to a suspected witch as "an old lady." The term dókeniŋk is always translated by the Winnebago as "old lady," and is quite different from the literal term hinωkš²ak, "old woman," which is seldom used.

5. The Winnebago ceded their homeland, which comprised most of southern Wisconsin and the northwestern corner of Illinois, in the course of three treaties with the government in 1829, 1832, and 1837. The tribe maintained that the last treaty was signed under duress, was misrepresented to them, and was signed by unauthorized tribesmen. Part of the tribe felt that they were ·outnumbered and outarmed and the best course was to submit to the terms of the treaty. They accordingly moved to a reservation in Iowa, but in 1846 were moved to another reservation in northern Minnesota. In 1855 they were again forced to cede their land and were moved to a reservation in southern Minnesota where they exhibited a remarkable willingness to become acculturated and accept a farming economy. They anticipated receiving patents in fee to plots unofficially distributed among the families by their agent. However, the Sioux uprising in Minnesota in 1862 was used as an excuse to force their removal from their improved lands although as a group they had taken no part in the uprising. They were taken to Crow Creek in South Dakota in cold weather and suffered great hardships and reduction in population. Fearing for their lives they fled down the Crow Creek to the Missouri River in dugout canoes.

Eventually, most of them settled among the Omaha in Nebraska. In 1865 they were allowed to exchange their Crow Creek land for a reservation in Nebraska along the Missouri River where about half of the tribe is presently enrolled.

Meanwhile, a part of the tribe consistently resisted efforts to remove them from the contested Wisconsin land involved in the treaty of 1837. Despite four removals by armed troops they always returned, their ranks swelled by dissatisfied members of the treaty-abiding faction. The last attempt to remove the Winnebago was made in 1874, the removal discussed by Mountain Wolf Woman.

6. The train stopped at Sioux City, Iowa, some distance east of the reservation where local Winnebago boarded the train to greet their kinsmen and ride the rest of the way with them to the reservation. The separation of families into reservation and nonreservation enclaves was a common occurrence and even today a great deal of visiting, intermarriage and residence shifts occur between the two groups.

7. This is the name of Mountain Wolf Woman's mother.

8. See note 3 above. These names could also be translated as Older Náqi and Younger Náqi, the former being the fourth son and the latter the fifth son. Occasionally people were known only by their sex-birth order names and Mountain Wolf Woman could supply no other names for these uncles.

9. After the removal of 1874 the government stopped trying to keep the Winnebago out of Wisconsin and allowed them to take up forty-acre homesteads which were to be tax-free and inalienable for twenty years. Most of these homesteads have passed from Indian ownership through sales or tax default and the remaining ones are of little use agriculturally since they have been divided into ever smaller parcels through inheritance over several generations. The land itself was for the most part rather poor and the Wisconsin Winnebago used the homesteads as headquarters where they planted gardens but which they abandoned for long periods to hunt, trap, or gather wild foods. Often they found the timber stripped from the land by whites during their protracted absences. Gradually, the Wisconsin Winnebago formed settlements of a few dozen to several hundred people near white communities throughout central Wisconsin from Wittenberg on the east to La Crosse on the west. The settlements are located on mission lands, government lands, or lands bought or rented by the Winnebago.

10. Allotment in severalty was carried out on the Nebraska reservation some time after the removal of 1874, but enrollments were made as early as 1865 with the understanding that this land would be secured to the Indians without further removals. Hence the advice of Mountain Wolf Woman's uncle to her father to register and assert his claim to Nebraska land.

11. This argument was frequently voiced by members of the Thunder Clan who felt that land matters were the exclusive concern of Bear Clan people who would act in the interests of the entire group.

12. Although the Winnebago ideally practiced both clan and moiety exogamy, this account indicates that the custom was not always observed as early as the 1860's. Both of Mountain Wolf Woman's parents belonged to the upper or bird moiety although they were of different clans.

13. Like many American Indians the Winnebago considered tobacco a sacred plant, using it in propitiation of the spirits and as proper remuneration for goods and services of a supernatural nature.

14. Woengáire, to give away, relates to the idea that highly valued possessions are given away rather than saved. Thus, children may be given away in the sense of honoring rather than rejecting the child. Sometimes a child is requested because he reminds a bereaved parent of a dead child and such requests cannot be refused. In any case, the child usually continues to live with his own parents but may claim certain benefits from the person to whom he is given as well as acquire certain obligations toward that person. In the instance noted, the child herself became, in effect, the payment for her own cure, the most precious object her mother could tender. The story indicates the esteem in which she was held.

15. A number of highly esoteric concepts are involved in the old woman's statements. "You have made me think of myself" is a direct translation of the Winnebago, and expressed in English in these same words by both Mountain Wolf Woman and my translator, Mrs. Wentz. The phrase suggests both the sense of being honored and the sense of pondering the meaning of one's own existence. Any gift, furthermore, carries the requirement of a return gift of equal value. Therefore, the old woman cured Mountain Wolf Woman not by the usual and simpler expedient of herbal medicine alone but by the proffer of her own life and longevity. The basis of her statement is the fundamental belief

that the proper life span of a human being is one hundred years. Thus, at wakes the deceased is asked to distribute among his relatives his unused portion of good things from his remaining years. The old woman made this type of bequest but the statements also carry the implication that she is able to share the force of her personal power before her death. Finally, the bestowal of a name from her clan implies benefits to the recipient of the name. Clan names are sacred in nature and given lists of names are the property of each clan. The name signifies the protection of the clan spirit. Mountain Wolf Woman never received a name in her own clan, the Thunder Clan, but was reckoned as a member of her father's clan rather than the Wolf Clan. The name, Xeháćiwíŋga may be analyzed as follows. Xe: mountain, hill or bluff; haci: to live in or make a home in; wiŋ: denotes a female name, often translated as "woman"; ga: referent suffix.

16. The suspicion that one is envied is a typical Winnebago reaction in explaining another's displeasing behavior. Illness and bad luck are also considered evidence of witchcraft on the part of someone who envies a person's health and good fortune. Presumably Mountain Wolf Woman had the blessings of two clans since she was a member of one clan and had a name from another clan, sufficient reason to be envied.

☖ NOTES TO CHAPTER II

1. The discussion of trapping and digging yellow water lily roots along the Mississippi River was recorded on a final reel of tape to be inserted here. There are several species of yellow water lily and so the plant known as ćerap among the Winnebago can only be identified in this connection as belonging to the genus Nuphar.

2. The single term hoćox used in this statement carries the con-

notations of both warding off bad luck and bringing good luck. The Winnebago observe a number of prenatal taboos relating to the health and personality of the child after birth, but the custom noted in this context refers to the belief that pregnant women must take special precautions to protect the fetus when engaging in unusual activities such as wading in search of *ćerap*. There is also a general feeling that pregnant women are apt to be unsuccessful in such quests unless they take such measures. Mountain Wolf Woman found this incident very amusing and laughed when she heard it played back on the tape.

3. The translation of the description of how Mountain Wolf Woman's father dug a well is far from precise. It became apparent to Mountain Wolf Woman that I was completely lost in trying to follow the Winnebago narrative and she inserted English words and gestures in order to clarify it for me. The result was that neither Mrs. Wentz nor I could get anything more than a general impression of the appearance of the well from the account on the tape.

4. The appearance of the woods reflects the fact that the Winnebago formerly burned out the underbrush in order to encourage the growth of blueberries. When they were forbidden to do so by the Wisconsin Department of Conservation they complained that the underbrush was a cause of forest fires or at least their rapid spread and that they could no longer pick blueberries profitably as the plants were now choked out by underbrush.

5. This rather curious phrase is intended to imply that the Winnebago are always adaptable and self-sufficient, not that they traditionally sold blueberries to white people.

6. Apparently the plant described is *Apios americana*. The discussion of gathering Indian potatoes was recorded later and inserted at this place in the narrative.

7. The discussion of stealing beans from mice was recorded separately and inserted here. I have been unable to identify these beans as I have never seen them and verbal descriptions as "tan with specks" are too vague to be of much help. It is possible that these beans were never gathered in Wisconsin but represent an activity peculiar to Nebraska since all accounts that I have obtained refer to Nebraska.

8. That is, after the harvest and storage of garden produce.

9. The description of gathering cranberries is inserted here from a later recording. Mountain Wolf Woman decided to describe the seasonal cycle in detail after realizing that she had dis-

cussed a few of the seasonal food activities and omitted others, hence the frequent insertions of data in this chapter.

Although the Winnebago had picked cranberries for many years to sell to white people, by the time Mountain Wolf Woman was a child, cranberry marshes were already being operated on a commercial basis by white owners who hired Indian laborers. The description of the work requires clarification. Formerly sections of marshland were drained off into ditches and became sufficiently dry for men to go through and rake the berries into containers and for women to sit on the ground gleaning berries after the raking process. This was the technique described by Mountain Wolf Woman and had been developed originally at the cranberry marshes in Massachusetts. About 1920 it was discovered that the Wisconsin cranberries, unlike those on the east coast, could remain in the water without harm right up to the time of harvesting from late September through October or until "freeze up time." The growers now surround sections of marsh with dikes, each section connected to the next by a water gate along the course of a creek. The water level in the marshes can thus be controlled and the harvest work is done entirely by men who wade through the water in hip boots. The berries are raked off the vines with a toothed scuttle implement and loose berries are caught in it as they float on the surface of the water. In this system women sort the harvested berries prior to shipment. However, this source of income is diminishing in importance for the Winnebago since machine operations have generally replaced hand labor since about 1950.

10. Informants ten or more years older than Mountain Wolf Woman recalled that in their early years the Winnebago still followed the tradition of eating only a morning and an evening meal. I believe that the change from two to three meals a day may be attributed to the fact that the Winnebago began to find employment as laborers for white farmers both in Nebraska and Wisconsin and took their meals with the farm families. Habits learned at boarding schools no doubt reinforced the change.

11. This statement illustrates a recurrent theme, concern for precision of amounts, distances, directions, and size. Mountain Wolf Woman is saying, in effect, that she must have been very young not to know exactly how much was earned.

12. A Jewish peddler.

13. Today when wigwams are used for ceremonies they sometimes become very smoky and the older people make a point of chid-

ing the younger people that they are losing the art of building wigwams. A number of younger people have said that wigwams were always smoky and that the older people have just become accustomed to living in houses where stovepipes carry off the smoke from wood-burning ranges.

❧ NOTES TO CHAPTER III

1. The reference is to family war bundle feasts. See Radin, "The Winnebago Tribe," Bureau of American Ethnology, Smithsonian Institution, *Thirty-seventh Annual Report* (Washington, 1915–16), 481–83, regarding ritual details. The above source is referred to hereinafter as Radin, BAE.
2. A single term, wopiŋkɛrɛ connotes the type of rack described and is compared to the sunshade described in context which is also connoted by another single term, haźacra.
3. Ideally a special feast was held to name a child, but children could also be named when a large group was gathered for some other purpose. The primary consideration was to broadcast the name widely when it was bestowed.
4. It is interesting to compare an account of the same incident as described by Brother Hágaga himself, *cf.* below. The autobiography of Brother Hágaga, named Big Winnebago, is entitled *Crashing Thunder,* and details concerning this matter may be found in Appendix B, a commentary comparing the two autobiographies. In my notes to each chapter, I refer to the writer of the autobiography as alias Crashing Thunder or Crashing Thunder, although Mountain Wolf Woman refers to him by his true name, Big Winnebago.

   "Five days before the feast was to be given I commenced to fast through the night also. On the fifth night, together with my older brother, I went to the feast. During the day I had

spent the time in the wilderness uttering my cry to the spirits:
'O Spirits, here humble in heart I stand,
beseeching you.'
I was far more thirsty than hungry. . . .
Our feast was given in a lodge that had eight fireplaces. The
host always sits near the last fireplace near the east end. There
we stood crying to the spirits. My older brother fell to the
ground from fatigue and exhaustion (pp. 80–81)."

There are some discrepancies in the versions of Mountain
Wolf Woman and her brother including the number of nights
he spent fasting and the number of fireplaces in the lodge. Most
notable are the different views of the older brother's attention
to sacred matters. Mountain Wolf Woman was no more than
eight years old and probably younger when the incident occurred since she speaks of her brother as a boy when he fasted
and he was about ten years her senior. It is possible that the
younger brother was sent back to continue his fast which caused
him to faint. Mountain Wolf Woman was only impressed by the
difference in attitude between the two brothers concerning sacred activities and the fact that her mother was very distressed
by Hénaga's behavior generally in regard to religious ob-
servances.

5. Nephews (the real or classificatory sisters' sons) of a man who
is giving a feast or other ceremony are traditionally called upon
to render assistance.
6. Boys no longer fast. However, feasts of this type are still held
in Wisconsin.
7. Girls fasted without the specific intention of the vision quest
although occasionally they were so blessed. The basic idea was
that such appeals to the spirits would reward girls in a general
way with a long and useful life, a good husband, and a large
family of healthy children.
8. The spirits had pity or compassion for the supplicants and
would bestow blessings.
9. A government boarding school was once operated for Indian
children at Tomah, Wisconsin. It was later turned into an Indian hospital and, about the time of World War II, was taken
over by the Veterans Administration as a veterans' hospital.
10. This phrase connotes isolation for four days and nights.
11. Mountain Wolf Woman considered this a prophetic dream and
not a vision as in the boy's quest for a guardian spirit. Most

vivid dreams or those which occur under exceptional circumstances such as during menstrual seclusion are considered as having some prophetic significance.

12. Mountain Wolf Woman recounted the long description of trapping muskrats and drying the pelts at this point. After listening to the playback of the tape she felt that the seasonal cycle ought to be considered as a unit. The trapping and water lily gathering episodes at the Mississippi River were accordingly placed in context in the foregoing chapter.

13. The bark-covered cabins, rectangular with gabled roofs, are connoted by the single term cióse. By the time Mountain Wolf Woman was a child the Winnebago no longer made such dwellings although they were still in use among the Potawatomi in Wisconsin. Cióse is a Winnebago word and Mountain Wolf Woman was told that they were once made by the Winnebago. The earth-covered roof upon a layer of hay was considered a means of keeping such dwellings cool in the summertime.

14. Actually a rather remote parallel cousin of Mountain Wolf Woman's father. The exact degree of relationship is unknown to Mountain Wolf Woman except that the woman was her classificatory "aunt."

15. In the English version of this incident Mountain Wolf Woman added that besides the bag of maple sugar cakes, her parents were also given a flour sack half full of powdered maple sugar. Mrs. Wentz observed that it is typical of the Winnebago to recall a gift of maple sugar even after many years have elapsed. It was and is a highly valued commodity.

16. Although the relationship is remote, knowing the term by which she addressed her son-in-law's father's mother's mother allows Mountain Wolf Woman to work out the variant relationship in which she stands to her son-in-law. Many older Winnebago, particularly women, enjoy tracing out such patterns of relationship although in practice the closer relationship determines the behavior observed. Mountain Wolf Woman observed traditional avoidance regarding her oldest daughter's husband and mentioned that when he came for her to assist his wife in the delivery of her child she was embarrassed to be seen riding in the same automobile with him. Although she claims that she no longer observes these traditional behaviors, I have noticed that she maintains a certain aloofness and avoids unnecessary conversation even with her youngest daughter's husband.

17. The term "their son" is a literal translation. In English, he

would be their nephew. Among the Winnebago, siblings of the same sex call one another's children by the same terms they call their own sons and daughters. Rattle Snake, mentioned somewhat later in this chapter, is another brother of the two old men, while a fourth brother, Snake Chief, was High Snake's real father. High Snake's own name is literally "Lies High," but because it is a Snake Clan name, it is always translated into English as High Snake.

.18. When Mountain Wolf Woman made this statement there was a tone of nostalgic affection in her voice, recalling a group that is long since gone, who dressed and behaved in traditional Indian fashion.

19. Slippery elm bark is a laxative and was bought from the Indians by wholesale drug suppliers.

20. According to *Crashing Thunder* (pp. 138–40) the troupe of dancers went to St. Paul. He mentioned in this connection that he learned to ride a bicycle at that time but made no note of having sent a bicycle to his sister.

21. This was a social dance, purely a matter of in-group entertainment and with no ceremonial purpose. The translation of the women's dance as the "squaw dance" is generally used among the Winnebago with mildly humorous intent.

22. "Citizens' clothing" is the translation supplied by Mountain Wolf Woman for the phrase which literally means "I made myself into a white person." The term "citizens' clothing" reflects the influence of the Indian Bureau during the period when the *Annual Reports* of the Commissioner of Indian Affairs often contained statistical tables for each tribe noting the number of men who had cut their hair, the number of people who had abandoned Indian styles of dress, etc. The term was doubtless familiar to Mountain Wolf Woman because of her two years at the government school at Tomah. Mountain Wolf Woman's appearance struck an entertaining note of incongruity at the dance since the rest of the people were dressed in typical Winnebago finery for the occasion.

23. "They liked it for me" is a literal translation employed by both Mountain Wolf Woman and Mrs. Wentz. The implication of empathy in another person's pleasure is contained in the alternative translation of hiŋǵipinʌ as "they liked it when I enjoyed myself."

❧ NOTES TO CHAPTER IV

1. In addition to causing her brothers embarrassment, to go against their wishes would be breaking a taboo and they would suffer for it.

2. Among the Winnebago, marriage was a purely secular contract symbolized in the exchange of goods between the couple's parents. The bride brought clothing and female finery for her mother-in-law to distribute among the female relatives. The groom returned with horses, occasionally even a wagon or buggy, and clothing and jewelry contributed by his female relatives, particularly his sisters. A larger amount was given by the groom's family and the wealth of goods was a measure of esteem in which they held the daughter-in-law.

3. The bride returns to her home with the goods received from the groom's family. Often a young couple remained with the wife's family for a time so that the groom could work for them to further increase the size of the bride-price in service. They usually left when they began to have children and thereafter residence tended to be patrilocal, either with the groom's family or near his home.

4. Mountain Wolf Woman was so angry about the marriage arranged for her that she vowed that her children would choose their own mates, which they did. However, the marriages of her two older daughters by her first marriage were carried out with a traditional gift exchange after the young people had made their own decision to marry. Mountain Wolf Woman did try to discourage some unfortunate matches among her children but did not enter into any prior arrangements for them although she was approached by the parents of prospective spouses for her children.

5. Mountain Wolf Woman justifies leaving her husband on grounds that are eminently acceptable among the Winnebago:

he was a jealous man. *Cf.* Radin, BAE, 175, regarding instructions given to sons: "My son, this also I will tell you. Women can never be watched. If you try to watch them you will merely show your jealousy and your female relatives will also be jealous. After a while you will become so jealous of your wife that she will leave you and run away. . . . You yourself will be to blame for this. . . . Everyone will consider you a very bad man."

6. The membership of the medicine lodge is divided among five bands, each occupying its own place in the lodge during the ceremonies. The actual location of bands depends on which band is acting as host. When a new member is initiated to replace a deceased member a sixth band is formed temporarily to deal with the transfer of membership and paraphernalia and has its special place. See Radin, BAE, 350–78; and Radin, *Road of Life and Death* (New York, 1945), *passim,* for detailed accounts of the ritual and cosmology of the medicine dance.

7. The initiate is usually presented with a complete outfit of Indian style clothing. Mountain Wolf Woman was asked to sew such a costume but did not know that it was for her own eventual use.

8. In the family's place in the medicine lodge.

9. The terms of address for parents-in-law are the same terms used for grandparents and the usual reciprocal terms for these in-laws are the equivalent of daughter-in-law or son-in-law (new woman, new man). However, when a bond of affection exists or the parent-in-law wishes to stress such a bond, the reciprocal term in the sense of grandparent is used. Thus, Mountain Wolf Woman is addressed as granddaughter in this situation.

10. The recollection of this sensation reflects the fearful awesomeness in which the rite was held by the uninitiated, despite the fact that in time Mountain Wolf Woman was disillusioned about the rite.

11. Mrs. Wentz stopped translating for a moment when she heard Mountain Wolf Woman's mimicry of her mother-in-law's plea and said, "She could hardly refuse such a request!" The Winnebago still feel a strong compulsion to fulfill requests, even distasteful ones, and Mrs. Wentz, who is not yet thirty years old, identified spontaneously with the difficult position Mountain Wolf Woman found herself in over fifty years ago. Mountain Wolf Woman's comments clearly illustrate the contrast between overt and covert patterns of behavior wherein she fulfills the requirements imposed by her culture while reducing the sense of

personal tension these requirements produce in given circumstances.

12. The reference to her parents' departure for Nebraska was contained in the earlier reference to leaving her husband (see note 5 above). Mention was made of the powwow at Black River Falls but in mid-sentence Mountain Wolf Woman decided to include the medicine dance episode. Although Mountain Wolf Woman contemplated leaving her husband, she apparently did not intend to rejoin her family of orientation and thus remained in Wisconsin rather than find an excuse to leave in the desire to accompany her sick father. The reference to Nebraska is worth special attention. Although the wording seems to imply the influence of nineteenth century medical ideas about "a change of air," the pattern of flight from unpleasant circumstances is a familiar problem-solving device among the Winnebago. Mountain Wolf Woman's narrative provides frequent illustrations of this.

13. The Winnebago community at Black River Falls, Wisconsin, is actually located some seven miles east of the town where an Evangelical and Reform mission was established in 1874. The powwow ground is about a mile from the mission buildings. There has long been a clustering of Winnebago dwellings in the immediate area of the mission as well as a scattering of homes for a radius of several miles around the mission nucleus.

14. While Mountain Wolf Woman was married and living at Wittenberg, her brother Big Winnebago, alias Crashing Thunder, was being held in jail on suspicion of murder (Radin, *Crashing Thunder,* pp. 159–67). Although she admitted to questions by Paul Radin that she had accompanied her parents on a visit to the jail, when she reached this point later in the transcription of her autobiography she made no mention of it. I personally doubt that she felt much concern for her brother although it was a situation fraught with dramatic pathos for him by his own account. She is long since reconciled with this brother, but her bitterness about his arranging her marriage and her anger with him, even after these many years, were strikingly apparent in her voice and manner as she recounted the story of her marriage.

15. The proper name of this ceremony is the Night Spirit Dance but it is generally known as the sore eye dance, supposedly because the active dancing involved kicks up a lot of dust and

leaves the participants with sore eyes by the time morning rolls around.

16. Mountain Wolf Woman expressed some concern that this rather humorous incident might antagonize members of the medicine lodge, but she decided to let it remain in the narrative since it was something she actually saw. This was the only incident in the entire narrative she even contemplated deleting once it had been transcribed.

17. Red Horn, by the reckoning given, is Mountain Wolf Woman's brother-in-law and therefore she could treat him in this fashion, since they would stand in a joking relationship. Red Horn's wife, Wave, remained at home with her child because it was considered dangerous for children to be near the medicine lodge when rituals were in progress.

18. Although Mountain Wolf Woman's brother was already living with Four Women and Mountain Wolf Woman refers to her as her sister-in-law, alias Crashing Thunder belatedly decided to formalize the marriage by an exchange of gifts, requesting a horse from his relatives for this purpose. The sister-in-law, in turn, gave Mountain Wolf Woman a traditional gift of clothing and jewelry.

19. Bad Soldier, a Bear or Soldier Clan name, signifying a fierce soldier. The Bear Clan acted as a police force in the village and on the march in hunting and warfare.

20. The English version makes explicit Mountain Wolf Woman's rationalization for marrying a married man: "But my brother, he want me to marry him." Obviously, she was no longer bound as strongly by her brothers' wishes in such matters but she felt her oldest brother, the true Crashing Thunder, had a more valid reason for arranging a match (to be able to visit her since it would be improper to visit a sister who lived alone) than had Big Winnebago, who merely wished to discharge a debt of gratitude incurred while he was drunk. Although Mountain Wolf Woman had told me of her two marriages, I had not been aware that the second was a legal marriage. Few women of Mountain Wolf Woman's generation were married according to American law and since it is now a rather delicate topic I never asked about it. Since her second husband had no family to provide a traditional gift exchange to establish a proper contract in Winnebago opinion, Mountain Wolf Woman was impressed by the sincerity of Bad Soldier's intentions in offer-

ing a legal marriage: "He want to be sure that he's going to marry me. He want to make a legally married to me."

As noted in Appendix A, Mountain Wolf Woman's sister Hinákega, who was childless, kept the two daughters of Mountain Wolf Woman's first marriage. Mountain Wolf Woman's husband once asked her to look after his daughter by his first marriage in any way that she could, and a warm relationship exists between the two women, including instances of mutual aid.

❧ NOTES TO CHAPTER V

1. Annuity payments from old treaties.
2. Mountain Wolf Woman wished to be with her sister while she was expecting a baby. Her husband stayed behind to earn more money before joining her in Nebraska.
3. The peyote religion, chartered as the Native American Church, combines Christian symbolism with peyote taken in the nature of a sacrament. Peyote is a southwestern cactus (*Lophophora williamsii*) which produces auditory and visual hallucinations. The tops of the cactus which are eaten are referred to as "buttons." For general descriptions of the diffusion and historical development of the peyote religion see J. S. Slotkin, *The Peyote Religion* (Glencoe, Illinois: The Free Press, 1956). Slotkin devotes particular attention to the role of the Winnebago in the development and diffusion of the peyote religion.
4. The long section ending with the sentence, "I even saw Jesus!" is inserted at this point at Mountain Wolf Woman's request. I asked her how she happened to accept peyote as a religion in addition to employing it for purely medicinal purposes. She began to tell me about it and then decided we ought to record it and insert it in the narrative at this point. This is the only instance that I exerted a conscious influence on Mountain

Wolf Woman to recite matters which she had repressed in the course of free associational narrative. Two factors seem to explain her initial reluctance to discuss her religious conversion in terms of a startling vision.

First, Paul Radin questioned her about peyote before we reached this point in her account. Since he spoke of her brother's first vision in what she considered an offhand manner, she did not want to speak of a matter of such deep emotional significance to herself. Dr. Radin expressed mild amusement that her brother's first vision had included frightening snakes, so she confined herself to telling him a funny incident in regard to an early peyote experience. She had had an argument with her husband and had left him briefly, but shortly thereafter she attended a peyote meeting and repented of her action to which she testified publicly. Later, an old woman came up to her saying she had been married many times but had never felt compelled by peyote to return to any of her husbands. Mountain Wolf Woman does not include this incident in her narrative.

Second, she feared that when her story was published some nonpeyotist Winnebago might read it and make fun of her for thinking of herself as an angel.

5. This statement requires comment since Mountain Wolf Woman has presented a somewhat general reference to personality changes. If observation of Winnebago women since 1944 is any clue to earlier conditions, overt traits of personality shift as a woman matures. Young women were ideally shy, but unmarried girls of today and even Mountain Wolf Woman in her day cannot be described as exactly retiring. However, young married women of today, even those who were quite outgoing when they were single, tend to be somewhat reserved and even bashful. As a woman's children grow older and particularly after she has grandchildren, she becomes more confident and outspoken. As a matter of fact, the young matron has a rather difficult existence. Unmarried girls find prestige in being sought as marriage partners, and older women are able to take more part in traditional religious activities as well as learn about medicines. Age is still generally respected despite Mountain Wolf Woman's opinions about the younger generation's attitude. The young matron has the responsibilities of caring for children, often experiences anxiety about holding her husband as youth and beauty wane and he becomes bored

with domesticity, and is likely to feel some strain in relation to her in-laws. It appears she is consequently more self-conscious about creating a good impression in her community by conforming to Winnebago traditions; that is, she should be reserved, respectful of older people, quiet and industrious. When I first noticed age differences in female personality I attributed the young matrons' behavior to the strains of acculturation not experienced by older women and not appreciated by single girls who do not have to worry about feeding a family in an economic world controlled by white people. However, observation of the group over a period of years revealed changes of behavior among women who were beginning to have grandchildren.

6. As noted in earlier chapters, the Winnebago have long followed a seasonal itinerary to pick produce of various sorts for white employers. Notions of higher or lower status in the relationship do not exist for the Winnebago who look upon the relationship as complementary. They can work or not work as they choose and verbalize this as, "I like to be my own boss." In the opinion of many Winnebago the responsibilities and deferment of rewards involved in ownership or control of fields and orchards far outweigh any advantages of proprietorship. Varied work and immediate rewards are considered preferable. Thus, in saying that they were merely making money for the white people, Mountain Wolf Woman meant not only their creditors but the white employees her husband paid on a piecework basis during husking time.

7. Mountain Wolf Woman discusses the custom of adoption in greater detail in the English version. "There was some nice family and they lost a daughter. When they see me they thought of their daughter, they says."

8. In retrospect Mountain Wolf Woman saw that she presented a rather ridiculous picture and as she recounted this incident she mimicked her tearful scolding, making clear that she really did not have a just complaint.

9. While I have long understood Winnebago economic attitudes as set forth in note 6 above, as I heard this statement I automatically assumed that Mountain Wolf Woman regretted spoiling her husband's vocational opportunities. When we began translating the tapes together, I was chagrined to discover no such regret was expressed and I should never have expected it. The conflict was a purely Winnebago one, the opportunity for

in-group prestige in learning another Indian language against the always strong bonds of family associations.

10. Thomas Roddy, a native of Black River Falls, used the name White Buffalo and took troupes of Indian dancers about the country as entertainers, as noted. His comments on peyote are recorded in Appendix B of Emma Helen Blair (ed.), *Indian Tribes of the Upper Mississippi Valley and Region of the Great Lakes* (2 vols.; Cleveland, Ohio, 1911–12), II, 281–83 and 298. He noted the opposition to peyote and the large gathering of Nebraska peyotists in Wisconsin in 1908. In the same volume a letter from Jacob Stucki, missionary to the Winnebago at Black River Falls (pp. 297–98), discusses the same delegation placing the number of visitors at 100. In 1958 Mountain Wolf Woman financed a peyote meeting in commemoration of the fiftieth anniversary of the introduction of peyote into Wisconsin.

11. The Frog Place was located along the Morrison Creek near the Indian mission and was so named because here the Chippewa gathered with the Winnebago to dance the Drum or Dream Dance. Their singing sounded like the croaking of frogs to the Winnebago. Mountain Wolf Woman recalled that these visits included the exchange of gifts (blankets and horses for Chippewa beadwork) and were common in her childhood. The last gathering occurred in 1920.

12. At this point Mountain Wolf Woman made a side remark in English, laughing as she did so: "We should have beat them up but we didn't." Peyotists can become rather saccharine, bewailing their "martyrdom" and making a great point of accepting the philosophy of turning the other cheek, matters which Mountain Wolf Woman can view in refreshingly realistic perspective.

13. Guide, that is, a functionary in charge of seating arrangements, etc.

14. When Winnebago men fight among themselves, an effort is made to disfigure opponents rather than simply hurt them. Cf. Thomas L. McKenney and James Hall, *The Indian Tribes of North America*, eds. F. W. Hodge and D. I. Bushnell (3 vols.; Edinburgh, 1934), II, 299, in regard to an incident of nose-biting among the Winnebago in 1846. The blow to a man's vanity (an important consideration among Winnebago males) was doubly disgraceful if his nose was bitten. A man not only became ugly but appeared somewhat ridiculous since husbands traditionally punished unfaithful wives by biting or cutting

off their noses. Thus, when the intruder at the peyote meeting accused the speaker of biting noses he was making a serious charge. The restraint of the speaker in laughing off the insult as only the meaningless teasing of an uncle is truly noteworthy as the exercise of Peyote-Christian forbearance.

15. In transcribing this section Mountain Wolf Woman mentioned several founders of the Half Moon rite by their English names, which are deleted as the implications are libelous. Later, Mountain Wolf Woman provided a list of both Winnebago and English first and surnames of the twelve founders of the Cross Fire rite. The leader was John Rave whose Indian name was Beard and who was also known as Little Peyote Chief. She also listed the eight founders of the Half Moon rite and could give Indian names for all but three of them. None of the original leaders defected to the Half Moon rite although in one instance a son of one of the Cross Fire founders joined the Half Moon group. In both cases a single survivor remained from each of the original groups in 1959.

16. The implied point, made explicit in the English version, is that despite the controversial origin of the Half Moon rite, the young men who lead it today are responsible, self-supporting people. Mountain Wolf Woman's younger son has become active in leading Half Moon meetings which now include prayers and testimonials as well as singing. Cross Fire rites are still held occasionally in Nebraska. The names of rites derive from the arrangement of temporary altars. While the peyote religion includes no marriage ceremony, marital infidelity became a religious issue among the peyotists and illustrates Christian influences since traditionally Winnebago marriage was viewed primarily in secular terms. The peyotists also interdicted liquor and an early argument in their favor was that conversion to peyote meant renunciation of alcohol. This is no longer true, but old peyotists such as Mountain Wolf Woman are strictly opposed to drinking. Mountain Wolf Woman's attitude can be traced to her early observations of the unfortunate effects of drunkenness so that she never drank even before her conversion to peyote. Her religion merely reinforces her opinion on the matter.

❧ NOTES TO CHAPTER VI

1. The English term shack is used to describe a small, one-room dwelling which is not a wigwam. It does not carry derogatory connotations.
2. This phrase was spoken in English.
3. That is, Hínuga, the first daughter of a man named Laughs At Him. The discussion of events leading up to the old woman's death is rather confused in the Winnebago version because of a series of recording interruptions. I have used Mountain Wolf Woman's English version as a guide and rearranged the phrases in the Winnebago text according to the chronology of the English version.
4. I depended more on Mountain Wolf Woman's English version of this conversation than on the translation of the Winnebago version since the conversation was originally in English.
5. At this point I have deleted the English names. Throughout the rest of the story Mountain Wolf Woman uses more English names, an unconscious reflection of a practice which began to develop at about this point in the chronology of her narrative. It may be attributed largely to the fact that more people attended school where English names were used exclusively than was formerly the case. Throughout the rest of the narrative I have deleted English names and substituted descriptive phrases where Indian names were not also given unless the individuals were dead and the reference would not offend survivors.
6. A boarding school for Indian children established by the Evangelical and Reform Church and an extension of the work of the mission at Black River Falls.
7. The incident concerning Mountain Wolf Woman's granddaughter was recorded as an additional episode which she wanted to include at this place in the story.

8. The son and his wife were separated by the time their baby was born.

9. Although Mountain Wolf Woman had been opposed to the marriage, when her son married the girl, Mountain Wolf Woman presented her with some clothing as evidence of her recognition and acceptance of the match. Although it was only a token gesture of the custom of gift exchange, even such meager symbolization had largely disappeared by the 1930's when the incident occurred. Since legal marriages did not become popular as a substitute method of establishing the marriage contract, children are considered legitimate or illegitimate by the community in terms of length of common residence of the parents. In using the term daughter-in-law and in giving the young woman clothing, Mountain Wolf Woman establishes her grandchild as legitimate despite the short duration of her son's marriage.

10. Charles R. Lowe Cloud, self-styled "Indian Report," whose column, "Indian News," in the *Black River Falls Banner-Journal* won him a national reputation.

11. In the English version Mountain Wolf Woman mentions that she drove the child home in her car. She was one of the first Winnebago women to drive a car.

12. A government boarding school. In the course of my earlier field work Mountain Wolf Woman had explained her reasons for sending the girl away to school. She feared that she might die and that the child was becoming too dependent on her to manage for herself. She also feared there were too many temptations in the mission community for an adolescent girl. Finally, because Mountain Wolf Woman considered boarding school years as the happiest period in her early life, she wished to give her grandchild a similar experience.

13. Big Winnebago, alias Crashing Thunder.

14. Brothers-in-law and sisters-in-law stand in a joking relationship and are expected to engage in sexual joking that ranges from mild flirting to downright salaciousness. The entire incident reflects a number of typical Winnebago characteristics. Even among Christian Winnebago, it is not considered unusual that people who are about to die are able to foretell the future and that their spirits wander and communicate with each other before actual death occurs. The distinction between life and death is not considered a sharp division at least during the period immediately preceding and following death. Thus, when Mountain Wolf Woman's husband saw the shade of his sister-

NOTES TO PAGES 59–60

in-law at the door he greeted her in customary fashion by joking with her and treated the incident as a special case only in noting that she did not want to go away without him. Only the dying man could see the woman at the door.

15. The English word, undertaker, was used in the Winnebago text.

16. This incident is an interesting example of the complicated relationships among the Wisconsin Winnebago, the federal government and local white people. The nucleus of the Winnebago community at Black River Falls consists of a square of four forty-acre sections of land. One hundred and twenty acres belong to the Evangelical and Reform mission while thirty-nine acres in the northeast corner of the square belong to the federal government. This was an old Indian homestead lost through tax default (see Chapter I). A single acre was bought by an Indian family but the rest of the land remained unused for many years except for shacks built by Indians under the impression that they were on mission land where they were allowed to build dwellings. As a result of the depression of the 1930's, the federal government and Jackson County entered into an agreement whereby the land was given to the government if housing was provided for the Indians. The Indian Bureau then arranged for laborers from the Indian community to build Indian houses. Coincidentally, Mountain Wolf Woman chose to build on this land after the death of her husband and though she initiated the work and provided some of the lumber her house was the first one finished under the new provisions. The arrangements between the county and federal government were apparently known to the lumber dealer to whom Mountain Wolf Woman went to buy doors and windows. He referred Mountain Wolf Woman to the county judge, Harry Perry. Judge Perry acted in an unofficial liaison capacity between the Indians and their agent out of a sense of personal concern for the Indians. After Mountain Wolf Woman's house was built, two more dwellings in the same style were built beside it. Thirteen additional houses were built according to a different floor plan which included partial basements. None of the houses has plumbing. Water is supplied by government pumps located between every three or four houses. Electricity has been available since 1949 and the Indians have paid the cost of running lines to their houses although occupancy changes are administered by the government. Because Mountain Wolf Woman supplied most of her own lum-

ber and began her own building, she feels that she has a firmer title to her house than do the other Indians and thus resents being placed in the same category. Her final comment in this chapter reflects a common opinion about white officialdom. Generally the Winnebago have enjoyed friendship of a paternalistic and helpful nature from many influential white people in the area such as the late Judge Perry, Dr. Eugene Krohn who advised Mountain Wolf Woman to air out her house by rebuilding it, and Thomas Roddy mentioned in an earlier chapter.

17. A small private airport on the outskirts of Black River Falls.

✍ NOTES TO CHAPTER VII

1. The two incidents recounted in this chapter, learning about medicines and attending a scalp dance, were narrated together as a separate set of episodes after the bulk of the narrative had been completed. Mountain Wolf Woman wished to include them and we decided that since they occurred after the death of her husband we would put them in a special chapter at this particular place.

2. Mountain Wolf Woman was related to this man in two ways. The closer relationship was that of brother-in-law as he married two of her older sisters in succession. However, because of the disparity in their ages and because she desired to learn sacred information from him, she stressed the relationship of grandfather as connoting greater respect than the joking relationship of brother-in-law. The term grandfather is applied because he was the son of Mountain Wolf Woman's mother's father's father's brother. In English terminology they would be first cousins twice removed.

3. Literally, "about this big," with gestures showing a square about a foot and a half on a side.

4. An English-speaking person, i.e., average white American, would probably choose "three dollars" as a random amount to begin bargaining, but the Winnebago, like many American Indians, stress the number four.

5. This is more than a gratuitous bit of gossip. The neighbors, actually a niece of the old man and her family, probably had no objection to feeding the old man regularly. Mountain Wolf Woman doubtless seized on some casual remark so that the old man would not become so obligated to the niece that he would bestow on her the information Mountain Wolf Woman was seeking.

6. Mountain Wolf Woman outlines the traditional technique for obtaining favors. The gifts of clothing made it obvious that she was specifically interested in information concerning medicines. Gifts cannot be refused, and usually the recipient is aware that something is sought but will hold off in making the traditional request that the favor be named until he is satisfied that he is sufficiently recompensed for it. This is particularly true where medicines are concerned for their efficacy is impaired if the knowledge is gained too cheaply.

7. Although Mountain Wolf Woman is a peyotist and is convinced that peyote has great curative power, she looks upon peyote cures as a sort of last resort and in the nature of a miracle. Ordinary illnesses should be treated by ordinary methods. Furthermore, she looks upon Indian medicines as scientific despite many magical features in their use, and sees no conflict with her Christian or peyote beliefs.

8. Fourth Son, son of (Hínigra) Light At A Distance (Sáneiŋga—his mother's name), also called Spirit Man (Waŋkẇaxopíniga.) See Chapter VI. This is the same man who in his youth attempted to break up a peyote meeting and heckled a speaker about biting off people's noses. He remained opposed to Christianity and peyote to the end of his life and was regarded in the community with some awe as a member of the medicine lodge who probably knew bad magic as well as curative medicines. Membership in the medicine lodge does not necessarily mean an individual has knowledge of curative medicines. Furthermore, a nonlodge person may become a healer in the fashion noted by Mountain Wolf Woman.

9. In addition to learning medicines from this grandfather, Mountain Wolf Woman acquired additional information from various sources, on one occasion paying for a specific medicine with

135

two tanned buckskins that she might have sold for about $7.00 apiece. Mountain Wolf Woman was also a midwife until well into the 1930's when Winnebago women began going to hospitals as a matter of course. Between 1944 and 1946 Mountain Wolf Woman was also the "health officer" at the mission, reporting the occurrence of illnesses, particularly infectious diseases of children, to the county public health nurse. These manifold roles as healer are indicative of the weighing of relative merits in white and Winnebago culture that characterizes Mountain Wolf Woman's adaptation to her social environment. An interesting incident occurred in 1949 when Charley Lowe Cloud (see Chapter VI, note 10) was dying of cancer and Mountain Wolf Woman had him taken to the clinic at Black River Falls to be cared for. Before the ambulance arrived she went to his tarpaper wigwam, bathed him and had him put on a clean set of long underwear that she had brought, the usual nightwear of old Winnebago men. She was concerned for the patient as her uncle, but also concerned that he should be neat and clean when he entered the hospital and give the hospital personnel a favorable impression of the Indians.

10. I have inserted the term "old religious ways" since Mountain Wolf Woman used only the referent form, " . . . when they spoke about that."

11. Usually when a scalp is brought back by a war party, in this case a German scalp from World War II, it is passed from one family to another and each holds a ceremony with it known as a victory dance. After the fourth such ceremony it may be put in the family war bundle or placed on a grave so the spirit of the scalped man will act as a servant of the deceased Winnebago in the next world. Thus the scalp in question had come back to or reached Mountain Wolf Woman's kin.

12. Formerly, a warrior gave his female relatives wampum or other objects of dress or adornment to wear in his honor at the victory dance. These might be trophies of war taken in the course of fighting or distributed among the warriors by the war leader to indicate feats of bravery performed. For many years, almost anything resembling clothing has been used for this purpose including blankets and yard goods and in this case a patchwork quilt cover that a woman can wear over her shoulders or about her waist.

13. The phrase *pinagigi* is translated as doing a kindness or as the

English words "thank you." Mountain Wolf Woman gave both alternatives in her English version of this conversation.

14. Mountain Wolf Woman's relationship to this man is adoptive and actually rather remote. She addressed him as déga, i.e., uncle, the term applied to a mother's brother and to his sons. This is a curious break in the symmetry of Winnebago kinship since all other cross-cousins are known by a special term best translated as cousin to distinguish them from parallel cousins who are addressed as siblings. In this case, Last To Emerge's (i.e., from hibernation, a Bear Clan name) father's sister died and so Mountain Wolf Woman's mother was adopted to fill her place. In English terminology they would be cross-cousins.

15. In the Winnebago version Mountain Wolf Woman merely says "those people," but in the English version she specifies them as "feaster people." By this she means non-Christian, nonpeyote Winnebago who often refer to themselves as "conservative." Old, unacculturated Winnebago are not familiar with this term and sometimes refer to themselves as "old time religion people" to describe adherence to traditional religious ways.

16. This man is a conservative and somewhat feared in the community since he is allegedly informed about bad medicines or witchcraft. He is the son of Mountain Wolf Woman's sister but he is only a few years younger than Mountain Wolf Woman. Although Mountain Wolf Woman is disdainful of the medicine lodge as "all make believe," like many Christians and peyotists she feels that the old religion was not entirely false but ineffective. In this incident she deplores the lack of reverence shown but is assured by her nephew that it is the formula, aside from questions of reverence, that brings results. Even this is disregarded today. Thus, a Christian who would observe the ritual properly can be rewarded. The nephew's own pragmatic outlook was reported conversationally by Mountain Wolf Woman. He thinks "maybe there is something to this Christian business" because once he prayed to Jesus all night for something as she told him to do and his wish was granted.

❧ NOTES TO CHAPTER VIII

1. Mountain Wolf Woman admitted that she wasn't certain of the current count of grandchildren and great-grandchildren, but had at least as many as noted.
2. The two daughters of Mountain Wolf Woman's first marriage were reared by her older sister who was childless, the same sister that helped Mountain Wolf Woman with the birth of her children.
3. Mountain Wolf Woman's first two daughters and her third daughter, the first daughter of her second marriage, were given names by Mountain Wolf Woman's father. Her first two sons who died in infancy had only their sex-birth order names and English names which she chose or agreed to have bestowed. Beginning with her third son, her children's Indian names are from peyote meeting bestowals in some cases. Thus, Lamb, literally Little White Deer, has Christian connotations. His English name was suggested by a white preacher. Sweet Corn and Swift Water's names were bestowed by their maternal grandfather. However, the name Sweet Corn was her grandfather's mother's name rather than a name from his own clan. The last three children have peyote names although the names are also old Winnebago names. The name Came On Earth or Stands On Earth in this case has reference to Jesus rather than the older connotation of Thunders. Mountain Wolf Woman gave all the English names of her children as she listed them as well as their Indian and sex-birth order names.
4. A doctor attended this birth.
5. Mountain Wolf Woman's oldest daughter attended this birth.
6. A doctor attended this birth.
7. Since the time of writing several of Mountain Wolf Woman's children have shifted residence.
8. This was the spring before the oldest grandchild by her second

marriage, who was reared by Mountain Wolf Woman, went to high school.

9. His attitude is decidedly "un-Winnebago," and Mountain Wolf Woman is preparing for the worst from a cowardly man.

10. The term can mean mother-in-law or grandmother. In the English version Mountain Wolf Woman uses the latter translation.

11. Her son's suggestion that he find work for her was intended and understood as thoughtful concern for her welfare. It enabled her to earn money and not be dependent on her daughter.

12. Mountain Wolf Woman is outgoing, friendly, and gregarious and indicates by this remark that though there were no other Indians about, she managed very nicely in a new situation.

13. Only the grandchild who went to Oregon with Mountain Wolf Woman returned to Wisconsin with her. I inquired about the baby who had been the reason for the long journey and Mountain Wolf Woman said matter-of-factly, "Oh, yes, she was born in July and I came to take care of the family when daughter went to the hospital."

14. "Old people" refers to Mountain Wolf Woman's sister and her husband. The daughter referred to is one of the two children reared by the above sister. Mountain Wolf Woman mentions later that she stayed at the tent of her sister at the medicine dance. Mrs. Wentz observed that participants at a medicine dance not only sit in the lodge according to specific groups, but camp outside the lodge at designated places in the order of their sitting arrangements inside the lodge. This is the same brother-in-law referred to by Mountain Wolf Woman in the preceding chapter as the person who used to invite her to feasts.

15. In the Winnebago version Mountain Wolf Woman neglected entirely the fact that her son eventually came home. I noticed this in going over the Winnebago tape and mentioned it. She therefore included a detailed account, inserted here, when she narrated the English version of the story. The omission apparently troubled her and she mentioned the extent of his wounds several times afterwards in the course of ordinary conversation.

16. A county social worker who, along with many other white people in the Black River Falls area, holds Mountain Wolf Woman in high regard.

17. This actually occurred after the girl at the window told her to sit down and wait. Mountain Wolf Woman had rather a long conversation with this person, a Yakima Indian man. She decided

to delete the conversation as he was very flattering about her making a long trip alone and seemed very interested in the fact that they were about the same age and both of their spouses had died. The incident was never taped.

18. In recounting this and other conversations which were held in English, Mountain Wolf Woman spoke in Winnebago. My translation has thus been guided in these instances by her English version.

19. In the English version Mountain Wolf Woman included a poignant account of her older grandson's departure for California: "We took him to Merrillan Junction, and he took the train. When he got in and was kinda weep, he had his suit case and then he had a handkerchief, and he wiped his eyes. Then my tears coming down already, part with my big boy."

The devotion of this grandson is reflected in the fact that he has taken her married name as his surname instead of using his father's surname.

20. Although Mountain Wolf Woman is deeply fond of all of her large family and endeavors to treat all of them with equal affection and fairness, she feels particularly close to the grandchildren whom she reared and who were old enough to appreciate that she had rescued them from being orphans. However, the total picture of family life through the years as described by Mountain Wolf Woman is characteristic of the Winnebago over at least the last two generations if not longer. People readily accept grandchildren, nieces and nephews and even unrelated children whose parents have separated, died or are unable to care for them. On one occasion a very remote cousin and his wife and children visited Mountain Wolf Woman. The couple had a quarrel and went their separate ways, leaving the children with Mountain Wolf Woman for several months. Eventually the father came back for them fully confident they had been well treated. He was annoyed, however, that Mountain Wolf Woman sold as junk the car he had left parked in her yard during his absence. She needed money to feed the additions to her family and when she did not hear from either parent for several weeks, she was resigned to keeping them indefinitely. She sold the car to provide funds until such time as she might be able to get Aid for Dependent Children payments.

21. Mountain Wolf Woman decided to accept one of these invitations at least temporarily, admitting that she is now old, but justifying her decision in the belief that she is needed. A letter

dated February 25, 1959, says in part: "I stop at [younger daughter's home] 2 or 3 days then I go back to . . . Waterloo Iowa. she want me there for good. because I'm old. of courst they all like to have me. either one. You too. but [older daughter at Waterloo] she left her girl in the morning when both of them they went to work. she gos to school 8 o.clock poor little girl by herself alone lost. that why she want me. I like it to."

22. The reference is to my work as a witness for the Winnebago in connection with their claim against the government before the United States Indian Claims Commission. My historical research, like my field work, preceded any claim work by several years. This work merely substantiated details of places and dates in regard to information known to the Winnebago. The Winnebago gave freely of their information before they or I had any idea that the collation of such data and the guidance it offered in checking historical sources would be of any future use to themselves.

⚘ NOTES TO APPENDIX A

1. This version was something of a tryout of the tape recorder technique so that the first half is particularly difficult to translate due to Mountain Wolf Woman's initial uncertainty with the microphone. By the time she began to speak of her marriage she felt at ease and no longer paused, repeated herself, or lost the thread of her discussion. Thus, my translation is primarily an effort to make her meaning clear rather than a close translation of her every word. This applies particularly to the section dealing with names of neighbors who lived near her parents' home.

2. This was said in English.

3. This is for my benefit, to make clear that she is referring to the older sister I knew.

4. We were interrupted at this point so that the naming of her children is a confusion of Indian names, English names and sex-birth order names. Since the matter is made clear in the long version I have simply deleted the listing.
5. An interruption occurred at this point so I have simply deleted a meaningless, unfinished phrase.
6. Literally, "You will rise." The connotation of leadership is supplied in Mountain Wolf Woman's English version of the event.
7. That is, be initiated into the rite rather than any literal connotation of making medicine.
8. The influence of white evangelism is apparent in Mountain Wolf Woman's English version of her peyote beliefs and practices:

   ". . . and so I used to pray, pray for everybody, pray for sickness, and pray for somebody died. Whoever relative died, I pray for them, and I help sickness. If I do good ways, I used to think that, that would be I have strength, my prayer be answered, and so is my weary ones get along good. Weary ones do the right way. That's what my belief is. . . . I expect to be see the eternal life."

   The Winnebago version is far more reminiscent of her mother-in-law's formal extolling of the merits of the medicine lodge.

NOTES TO APPENDIX B

1. Paul Radin, "The Autobiography of an American Indian," *University of California Publications in Archaeology and Ethnology,* XVI, 381–473.
2. Paul Radin, *Crashing Thunder* (New York, 1926).
3. Paul Radin, "Personal Reminiscences of a Winnebago Indian," *Journal of American Folklore,* XXVI (1913), 293–318.

Selected Ann Arbor Paperbacks
Works of enduring merit

For a complete list of Ann Arbor Paperback titles write:
THE UNIVERSITY OF MICHIGAN PRESS ANN ARBOR